LONGMAN IMPRINT BOO

Scenes fro

Key moments from world drama

Selected and edited by Michael Marland

General editor: Michael Marland
Series consultant: Geoff Barton

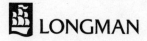

Longman Imprint Books
General editor: Michael Marland

New titles
Characters from Pre-20th-Century Novels selected and
    edited by Susie Campbell
Diaries and Letters selected and edited by Celeste Flower
Genres selected and edited by Geoff Barton
Highlights from 19th-Century Novels selected and edited by Linda Marsh
Landmarks selected and edited by Linda Marsh
Scenes from Plays selected and edited by Michael Marland
Stories from Africa selected and edited by Madhu Bhinda
Stories from Europe selected and edited by Geoff Barton
Ten Short Plays selected and edited by Geoff Barton
Travel Writing selected and edited by Linda Marsh
Two Centuries selected and edited by Geoff Barton

Previously published titles
Autobiographies selected and edited by Linda Marsh
Black Boy Richard Wright
Cider with Rosie Laurie Lee
The Diary of Anne Frank edited by Christopher Martin
Ghost Stories selected by Susan Hill
The Human Element and other stories Stan Barstow
I'm the King of the Castle Susan Hill
P'tang, Yang, Kipperbang and other TV plays Jack Rosenthal
A Roald Dahl Selection edited by Roy Blatchford
Stories from Asia selected and edited by Madhu Bhinda
Strange Meeting Susan Hill
The Woman in Black Susan Hill

Contents

Introduction — v

The Ants   1962 — 1
the radio play by Caryl Churchill

Separated Twins — 17
from the stage play *Blood Brothers*   1981
by Willy Russell

Who Is the True Mother? — 26
from the stage play
The Caucasian Chalk Circle   1954
by Bertolt Brecht

Death in the Barn — 45
from the television play
Blue Remembered Hills   1979
by Dennis Potter

Put the Old Man Away — 62
from the television episode *Homes Fit for Heroes*
in the series *Steptoe and Son*   1963
by Ray Galton and Alan Simpson

The Hundred Nights — 74
from the Japanese Noh play
Sotoba Komachi   14th century

Farewell to the Memories of Life — 82
from the stage play *Johnson over Jordan*   1939
by J. B. Priestley

Fighting Filth and Disease

from the stage play
An Enemy of the People 1882
by Henrik Ibsen

94

The Mystery of Goodness

from the libretto for the opera
Billy Budd 1951
by E. M. Forster and Eric Crozier

105

Death of a Martyr

from the verse play
Murder in the Cathedral 1935
by T. S. Eliot

119

Talk More Genteel

from the musical *My Fair Lady* 1956
by Alan Jay Lerner

125

Study activities 135

The authors 144

Further reading 150

Introduction

Human beings have made up and acted out plays all over the world ever since people came to live together in groups. Taking part in a performance as a member of the audience (and that *is* a form of taking part) is a powerful way in which people can feel part of things that have happened to others, to think about the events and emotions of life, and to extend their own understanding and feelings. From medieval European towns to African villages, from opera to television, from soap opera to verse plays, very many people have enjoyed and benefited from the art form of the drama.

This selection is of ten scenes from modern dramatic literature (and one early influence), including the founder of modern drama, the great Henrik Ibsen, with his *An Enemy of the People* of 1882. The scenes have been chosen to illustrate a range of drama in performance, using a variety of dramatic structures, different ways of portraying and interpreting character, different forms of setting and direction, and rich and diverse ways of using language. The range of forms and techniques includes the **epic theatre** of Brecht, the **realism** of Ibsen, as well as the **stylisation** of Eliot, scenes from the broadcast **media** of radio and television, from the fully or partly sung forms of **opera** and **musical**, a play written for a school hall to a play written for a cathedral.

Of course modern drama has its roots in the past – especially the ancient Greek theatre, the medieval European mystery play, the Renaissance drama of Spain and Elizabethan England, and the great Japanese fourteenth-century plays. In the 1920s and 1930s, stage directors and writers began to incorporate ideas and techniques from earlier forms, in particular those in which 'what happens next?' is not the overwhelming question as it is in a naturalistic television serial, for instance. One example of an earlier dramatic form included in this book is a scene from a Japanese Noh play. The Noh flourished initially in Japan in the fourteenth century, and is considered by some to be one of the great art forms of the world. The action does not take place before our eyes, but it is lived through by a character (in this case, the old woman, Komachi). It is a vision of life painted with the memories of the participant.

In the twentieth century the Irish verse writer W. B. Yeats was heavily influenced by Noh, as was the important stage director whose techniques were borrowed by so many across the world: Edward Gordon Craig (1872–1966). The musical composer Benjamin Britten (1913–76) was deeply impressed by Noh in Tokyo in 1956 and wrote a series of operas in which the narrative sequence is closer to Noh than to Ibsen.

There are two approaches to drama which have intertwined in the twentieth century:

- One is for the author and actors to make as close an imitation of real life as possible – that is the *naturalistic* approach. This is meant to make an audience think that what they are seeing could have actually happened just like this, with people speaking in exactly this way.
- The other is in which a performance is clearly presented as just that – a specifically devised set of movements and sounds which are not themselves real life but comment on and interpret life. This is best thought of as **stylised** or **symbolic action**.

Thus in this selection, the scenes from Henrik Ibsen, Ray Galton and Alan Simpson, and Caryl Churchill make us feel that we are listening to an actual event snipped out of a real sequence of life, one that could have taken place exactly like this. In these plays or these parts of plays the performance is written and directed to as much like a filmed documentary of real life as possible. However, the scenes by Bertolt Brecht, T. S. Eliot, J. B. Priestley and Willy Russell, for instance, are more like ballet or animated film: ideas extracted from life and re-created in a deliberately artificial way. It is as if at these times the writer is demonstrating points about life rather than merely asking the audience to watch life happening. These writers in these plays often create a way of speaking directly to the audience, not relying only on the dialogue of the action to express their views. Thus Mrs Johnston in *Blood Brothers* sings about herself directly to the audience just as the evil Claggart does in the opera *Billy Budd* and Higgins in *My Fair Lady* – all modern versions of the soliloquy in a Shakespearian play. At other times the voice of the play comes over directly through a narrator, as in *The Caucasian Chalk Circle*.

An important skill is dividing the story up into believable episodes. Ibsen developed the art of a continuous sequence that held the attention and seemed realistically to continue as if life was just happening. Modern writers, perhaps encouraged by the freedom of radio, film and television, have linked together smaller snippets of action, cutting from one to the other to compare and contrast different happenings in the story. Willy Russell's *Blood Brothers* chops from scene to scene on the stage as Dennis Potter's *Blue Remembered Hills* does on the television screen.

In all these scenes the central characters are very important, and one test of a good playwright is whether she or he, by whatever method, brings a convincing character to us. Thus, the after-life sequence of *Johnson over Jordan* is fantasy, but is the central character believable?

The scenes come from different forms, different countries and different decades. Yet some themes reoccur, of which one is the relationship between parents and their children. From Tim and his parting parents in *The Ants*, the first five scripts include a strong thread of this universal dramatic theme. Another group focus on one of the world's central dramatic concerns – the use and the abuse of power. We have to consider whether the characters with power are using that power properly and whether their opponents are attacking them fairly – with Thomas Becket in the twelfth century in *Murder in the Cathedral*, Stockmann in *An Enemy of the People* in the nineteenth century, and Captain Vere in *Billy Budd* in the eighteenth century.

In this collection literature in drama is represented by eleven scenes which take readers to the stages of the world to consider dramatic writing technique.

Michael Marland

The Ants

the radio play **by Caryl Churchill**   (1962)

Tim, a young boy, is staying with his mother, Jane, at his grandfather's house by the sea. Because this is a play written for voices and sounds to be heard through the radio loudspeaker, without the characters being seen, there are no stage directions. For instance, when Stewart and Jane return to the house (page 14), we do not read that on the page but can tell it from what Tim and Stewart say.

Tim is playing with some ants on the veranda, watched by his grandfather. The bomb mentioned is part of the Second World War, which is still continuing, though it seems very far away in this peaceful seaside place.

Characters

TIM
JANE, his mother
STEWART, his father
GRANDFATHER

TIM Hello, ant, what are you carrying? Is it something to eat? Is it? You're carrying something too, and you are, and you are, and you – here, don't stop. The others aren't stopping, you've got to get over to the other side of the veranda. What's the matter? Go on then. Where are you going? Along, along, into the crack. Into the crack and I can't see. They come out of it too. Here you, little one, you're smaller than the others, come on my finger, come on. Don't be frightened, don't run away. Come on, dear little ... There's another little one going the other way. You're little, you're little, you're middle, you're big. Big and shiny. What will you do if I put a twig in the way? You get over easily, don't you? Come on, you can, too. Come on, ants. (*Laughs*)

G'FATHER Well, there's another day over. It's six o'clock again. It always seems to be six o'clock now. Every day I notice when it's six o'clock and it means another day's over.

JANE (*Calls off*) Tim!

Pause

G'FATHER Tim, your mother's calling.

JANE (*Nearer*) What are you doing?

TIM Nothing.

JANE (*On the veranda*) Are you clean? Your father's going to arrive any minute, I don't want him to think I don't look after you. What's that? Ants? This house is disgusting, earwigs in the kitchen, there's something moving wherever you look. What do you do to ants, Dad?

G'FATHER Do you have to do anything?

JANE You can put petrol on them and set fire to it, can't you?

TIM No.

JANE Tim, go and get washed, dear.

TIM They're my ants. You're not going to hurt them.

JANE Wash your face and hands and comb your hair. And put on a clean shirt, and some sandals, what have you done with your sandals?

TIM You can't kill them, they're ants.

G'FATHER We won't touch them, Tim. Go and do what your mother says. Go on now.

THE ANTS

TIM (*Going off*) Daddy won't let you kill them.

JANE (*Calling after him*) Don't forget to comb your hair. You see? He plays us off against each other, 'Daddy won't let you.' It's as if he knew.

G'FATHER You can't expect him not to notice anything.

JANE But it's as if he's saying, 'If you're not nice to me you won't get custody of me, I'll go to Daddy.'

G'FATHER Won't that be up to the court?

JANE Yes, of course it will, I'm certain to get him. They can't take a child away from its mother.

G'FATHER I don't know about these things. Won't it depend on who they decide is the – what? The guilty party?

JANE Stewart's the guilty party.

G'FATHER What time is he coming?

JANE He's late.

G'FATHER You're looking very lovely. I haven't seen that dress before. Is there really any need to go so far as getting a divorce? (*Pause*) I suppose it depends on whether Stewart thinks you're looking lovely.

JANE It's all right for you to be sentimental, Father, it's not your life.

G'FATHER I just think you might as well settle for the mediocrity you know. The best you can hope for by leaving him is misery and tragedy and you probably won't even get that, you'll just be bored again.

JANE It's your fault I married him. You kept having him to stay, what could I do? I never saw anyone else.

G'FATHER You loved him.

JANE Oh, I don't know.

G'FATHER The thing is I find it very hard to care about you. It's hard enough to care about other people anyway, but when you get old and no one cares about you it's even worse. You're not the centre of anyone's life except your own, so there's nothing to make you notice other people. And if your head aches or your feet are cold, there's nothing as important as your feet and your head and your back.

Sound of car arriving

JANE Tim does love me, doesn't he?

G'FATHER I love you too. I think even Stewart loves you, you're a lucky girl.

JANE Well that was his car.

G'FATHER Go and meet him then.

JANE Yes. He'll come through to the veranda, I'll stay here.

G'FATHER Yes, lean on the rail, look out at the sea, ignore him. You look very nice like that.

TIM (*Calling*) Mummy, Mummy, Daddy's here.

JANE (*Loudly*) We're on the veranda, Stewart.

TIM Come on, Daddy. Here he is, Mummy. Look, he gave me some chocolate.

JANE Not before supper, Tim.

STEWART Hello, Jane.

JANE Hello, Stewart.

STEWART Good evening, Grandpa.

G'FATHER You used to call me Arthur and now you call me Grandpa. You've slipped two generations.

STEWART You're looking very well.

G'FATHER Nothing happens here. The days drop into the sea out there as they used to when you first came, plop, plop, as the sun drops into the horizon.

TIM Daddy, look at the ants.

STEWART Well, aren't they fine?

JANE Is that an evening paper, Stewart? Can I see it? We never seem to get a paper here.

STEWART Yes, of course. Here.

G'FATHER Yes, you forget there's a world outside and a war on. You can't imagine a war down here, but there's always one somewhere.

JANE They've dropped a big bomb.

THE ANTS

G'FATHER Which side?

JANE Us.

G'FATHER Dropped it on us?

JANE No, we dropped it.

G'FATHER I suppose that's just as well.

TIM Can you watch one ant, Daddy?

STEWART No, I lose track of them. They all look the same.

TIM I think there's one I know. He's a bit red. His name's Bill.

JANE Do you want to go for a walk before dinner, Stewart?

STEWART Yes, let's do that. Coming, Tim?

JANE I expect Tim wants to play with his ants.

TIM Yes.

STEWART Where shall we go then?

JANE Down to the sea?

STEWART In those shoes?

JANE I'll change them.

STEWART All right, be quick.

JANE I don't have to go upstairs. I've some sandals in the hall, come on.

They go off. GRANDFATHER *reads the paper.*

G'FATHER Ten thousand dead. Well. Typist to wed Maharajah. President's dog has puppies. Backs are in fashion. Duke jumps in fountain. My Desire at 100-1. Nothing in the paper. How's Bill?

TIM I'm not sure where he is just at the moment. I think he's gone under the wall, he'll be back in a minute.

G'FATHER Go on, you won't know him again.

TIM I will.

G'FATHER How did you meet him?

TIM He wandered away from the others, I nearly knelt on him, so I put him back.

G'FATHER What did he do then?

TIM He ran round and round as if he wasn't sure where to

go, and talked to some of the others about it, and then came down here. Look, there he is.

G'FATHER Are you sure?
TIM Yes.
G'FATHER What about that one?
TIM No, this one.
G'FATHER Where?
TIM Here – no, oh, where is he? Which one is he?
G'FATHER You can't tell one from the other.
TIM Oh – !
G'FATHER How many ants are there here?
TIM Millions.
G'FATHER Ten thousand?
TIM Yes, ten thousand. Is Daddy staying long?
G'FATHER I think he's here for the weekend.
TIM Till Monday?
G'FATHER Or Sunday night.
TIM Don't you know which?
G'FATHER Does it matter?
TIM I don't know. Can we give the ants something to eat?
G'FATHER Yes, I know, give them some sugar. I'll give them a teaspoon of sugar.

While he gets the sugar TIM *leans over the rail of the veranda.*

TIM I can see Mummy and Daddy on the beach. They can't see me, they're not looking. They look very small.
G'FATHER Here we are.
TIM Why doesn't Daddy come here for longer?
G'FATHER He's busy at the office all week.
TIM But he doesn't come every weekend.
G'FATHER Come and see the ants eating the sugar.
TIM (*Goes back to the ants*) Are we going home with Daddy at the end of the summer?

THE ANTS

G'FATHER Do you want to?

TIM I like the summer.

G'FATHER Look at them, they're just like people. Greedy, greedy. They don't know what to do, they didn't allow for that, ooh, isn't it nice. Look at them all telling each other about it, nasty, greedy things.

They're very intelligent, ants, as intelligent as people anyway. They've got everything organised, they all work together for their society. Look at them, tramp, tramp, back and forth, fetching and carrying, working for their living. Very smug they are about it, too. If an ant meets a grasshopper in the winter he says, 'What did you do all summer?' and the poor cold grasshopper says, 'I danced and sang in the sun', and the horrid self-righteous ant says, 'I worked hard so I've plenty to eat, you go to hell', and the poor grasshopper dies of cold and hunger.

TIM I like ants.

G'FATHER They've no imagination, just like people. Have you ever looked at a crowd of people? Run, run, run. Look at them from the top of a tall building some time, just funny patterns of people, or out of an aeroplane, funny little toy towns, coloured targets, and not even people then, just black ant motorcars.

TIM Have you been in an aeroplane?

G'FATHER Yes.

TIM Where did you go?

G'FATHER I came back to England.

TIM Where from?

G'FATHER New York.

TIM What were you doing in New York?

G'FATHER I really don't know.

TIM Was it nice in the aeroplane?

G'FATHER I didn't really notice.

TIM What's the point of being in it then?

THE ANTS

G'FATHER I was in a hurry.
TIM Why?
G'FATHER Your grandmother was dying.
TIM In the plane?
G'FATHER No, here in this house.
TIM Why wasn't she in New York?
G'FATHER She was in England.
TIM Was it a jet?
G'FATHER I don't think so.
TIM How many engines did it have?
G'FATHER I don't remember. You can't find Bill now, can you? Oh, I'm stiff. Oh. I'm an old man. I shouldn't get down on the ground like that. I should stay in my chair. Ah. (*He sits down*)
TIM When are Mummy and Daddy coming back?
G'FATHER Supper-time.
TIM I'm hungry. I can't see them, can you?
G'FATHER I wouldn't see them even if they were there, my eyes are too old.
TIM You aren't even looking.
G'FATHER I couldn't see them if I did look.
TIM I expect they've gone to the caves.
G'FATHER So we've dropped a big bomb.
TIM How big?
G'FATHER Very big.
TIM Did it kill a lot of people?
G'FATHER Yes.
TIM I expect it killed more people than any bomb's ever done before.
G'FATHER That's good, is it?
TIM You're meant to kill the enemy in a war.
G'FATHER Yes, that's true.
TIM Did you drop bombs out of your plane?
G'FATHER No.
TIM What did you do?

G'FATHER I read magazines.
TIM Is that when Granny died?
G'FATHER Yes, she died before I got back.
TIM I want my supper. (*He calls over the rail*) Mum-my! Dad-dy! I'm hun-gry!
G'FATHER They won't hear you.
TIM Is Uncle Peter coming this weekend?
G'FATHER No.
TIM When is he coming?
G'FATHER Do you like him?
TIM He catches a lot of fish.
G'FATHER Would you like him to be around all the time?
TIM Is he coming to live with you?
G'FATHER If he came to live with you.
TIM You live all by yourself.
G'FATHER Not at the moment.
TIM Do you like it?
G'FATHER I've got the ants for company.
TIM Mummy wants to kill the ants.
G'FATHER We won't kill them.
TIM How did she say do it? With petrol?
G'FATHER You pour petrol on and set light to it.
TIM Does petrol burn?
G'FATHER Yes.
TIM But it's wet. Does water burn?
G'FATHER No.
TIM If water burned you could burn up the sea. (*Pause*) What else can we do with the ants?
G'FATHER Why do anything with them?
TIM They're a bit boring just going up and down.
G'FATHER They don't know about you.
TIM They do if I give them sugar and put a twig in front of them.
G'FATHER They know sugar and the twig, they don't know you.
TIM I wonder where Bill is?

THE ANTS

G'FATHER They have terrible ants in foreign countries. They march in great armies, enormous ants eating their way through a jungle. They eat everything in their way.

TIM Would they eat you if you got in their way?

G'FATHER They might do.

TIM They wouldn't eat me, I'd stamp on them.

G'FATHER There'd be too many.

TIM I'd jump and jump.

G'FATHER Too many.

TIM I'd drop things on them.

G'FATHER There are too many. They make whole houses fall down. Locusts, too, great plagues of locusts stripping countries bare. Great seething masses of insects, you can't see any one of them, just masses and masses, destroying everything in their way. Think if you couldn't have any supper because the ants and locusts had eaten it all.

TIM I wouldn't let them.

G'FATHER Then try to stop them. Poor people run out with gongs and they beat and beat and beat to make a loud noise so the locusts won't come down on their crops, they run in the cornfields shouting and banging metal, but they do come down somewhere in the end.

TIM Do ants go away if you shout at them?

G'FATHER Try.

TIM (*Crouches down on the ground. Shouts*) Go away, ants. Go away.

G'FATHER Nowadays they're scientific, they spray the locusts and kill miles and miles of them. They fly up in aeroplanes and aim poison at them.

TIM What about ants? They don't go away when you shout.

G'FATHER I don't know what they do about them.

TIM You didn't mind me shouting, did you, ant? Come on my finger. There, where will you go on my hand? It's a long time since Daddy's been here.

G'FATHER He's very busy.

TIM Look, there's Bill. You come on my hand, too. Now he won't be lonely. What was your job?

G'FATHER Oh, I worked for a company like most people.

TIM Did you like it? (*To ants*) Come on.

G'FATHER No, it was a silly place. Like these ants in the city every day.

TIM Now I've got four on my hand.

G'FATHER They thought I was silly, too, so they sent me away in the end.

TIM (*To ants*) No, not up my arm, on my hand. They sent you to New York?

G'FATHER It was after that I went to New York, yes.

TIM Were you away as long as Daddy's been away? Come on, ants, come on my hand. Come on, more of you.

G'FATHER A bit longer.

TIM Didn't you like Granny any more? (*Pause*) Daddy doesn't like us.

G'FATHER Of course he does.

TIM (*To ants*) Not up my arm. Keep still. He doesn't live with us.

G'FATHER Would you rather live with him or Mummy?

TIM Yes, that's what they want to know. They're always going to live apart, aren't they?

G'FATHER Who would you rather live with?

TIM (*Suddenly, in horror of the ants*) Oh! Oh! Go away! Oh!

G'FATHER What is it?

TIM There were too many ants.

G'FATHER They won't hurt you.

TIM I don't like it, there were too many. I started out with one or two on my hand and I could see each of them all the time and one of them was Bill, and then suddenly there were lots of ants all over my fingers and up my arm and I couldn't tell where they all were, and I tried to knock them off my arm and they

THE ANTS

wouldn't get off and I couldn't tell where they were –

G'FATHER You've hurt them, you've squashed some of them.

TIM Oh! Do something.

G'FATHER Never mind.

TIM Do something. They're all squirming.

G'FATHER Stamp on them.

TIM No.

G'FATHER Stamp on them.

TIM No. You do it.

G'FATHER Like this. (*He stamps on the crushed ants, wipes his foot*)

TIM Ohhh.

G'FATHER Don't be silly. They're just ants.

Pause

TIM Can't I live by myself like you?

G'FATHER Not till you're older.

TIM When I'm older I don't want to live with anyone.

G'FATHER No, you remember that. You'll think you do some time, but remember what you said just now. You'll think you want to live with some girl and have lots of children and friends and jobs and live in a happy ant hill, but you don't, remember that. You want to be all by yourself and see the silly ants going up and down and give them sugar and stamp on them. Don't be fooled by love or vocation, you keep by yourself and you won't have to desert anyone later.

TIM What do you mean?

G'FATHER Desertion. Don't you know what desert is?

TIM Like pudding dessert?

G'FATHER No, like sandy desert. Desertion is me leaving your grandmother and your father leaving your mother. Desertion is when you stop loving people and see them from miles above, when you lose them and see just a lot of black ants.

THE ANTS

TIM   I don't know what you mean.

G'FATHER   And you know what adultery is? Not adult grown-up, adultery?

TIM   No.

G'FATHER   Adultery's Uncle Peter, and if you live by yourself you won't have that either. Live by yourself by the sea, remember that. You're edging away, to the rail. Yes, you watch the sea.

TIM   I don't know what you mean.

G'FATHER   I mean nobody loves anyone, that's what I mean. I'm an old man and it's all too late and nobody loves anyone. Out there they're all dropping bombs, bang, bang, bang, I don't know, I only know about me, I'm an old man and I'm stiff and cold, and none of us love each other.

TIM   Mummy and Daddy are coming. I can see them coming on the beach.

G'FATHER   Where?

TIM   (*Chanting with delight*) They're coming past the shrimping pools, they're climbing up the shingle.

G'FATHER   I can't see. She was such a pretty little girl too, she used to clamber all in and out of the shrimping pools. And he was such a nice boy when he came to stay here with us, and they'd go off down to the sea in the evening and I'd try not to watch because it didn't seem fair to watch, but I couldn't help it, I went all the way down to the sea with them, holding hands and kicking at the sand. I could feel the water round their ankles, though I was too far away even to see their ankles I suppose. We were so happy.

TIM   Mum-my! Dad-dy! Come on! Can't they hear me? They haven't even waved. Ooooheeee! Now Daddy's waving. Now Mummy's waving. Now they're in the sand-dunes, Mummy's slipping and Daddy's pulling her up, now they're coming. Now I can't see them, they've come on to the road. They're nearly here, they're just coming along the road. Why don't you look? They're at the gate, they're coming up the steps from the road. Here they are now, here they are! Daddy, Daddy –

STEWART Hello, Tim, hey, up you go. You're getting a heavy boy. Give us a kiss then.

TIM Mummy, hello, Mummy.

JANE Yes, Tim, all right. Don't jump like that, calm down, we've something to tell you.

STEWART Jane –

JANE Daddy and I have been having a talk –

STEWART Tim, listen, old man, it's like this. Mummy and I –

JANE I'm talking to him, you can't stop me, now be quiet for once.

TIM I saw you on the beach. I watched you coming.

JANE Tim, you already understand something of what's been going on, don't you? Though we haven't said anything about it.

TIM I saw you slip in the sand, did you see me?

STEWART Tim, I've been away a lot this summer, so I haven't seen as much of you as I wanted –

JANE You've liked this summer, haven't you, Tim?

TIM Yes.

STEWART But in the winter you may live with me or if you live with Mummy you'll see me a lot, won't that be nice?

TIM Yes.

JANE Tim, you know your father isn't living with us any more, and now we've decided for always he won't be living with us any more –

STEWART Jane, stop it, that's a mad way to do it.

JANE – and you're going to live with me and Uncle Peter.

STEWART Jane, will you be quiet.

Pause

TIM   Grandpa –
STEWART   Tim, listen to me a minute. It's not as bad as all that. It's fun, you'll have three houses to live in –
JANE   You're living with me. And you must tell anyone who asks you that that's what you're doing and that's what you want to do, do you understand? Now, who do you want to live with? With Mummy, don't you?
TIM   I want to live by myself.
STEWART   We're not sure who you'll be living with, Tim, but whoever it is you'll see the other one lots and lots, as often as you like, and you'll spend all the time you want by the sea with Grandpa –
JANE   Shut up! Tim, if they say do you want to live with Daddy, you must say no, because Daddy left us, Daddy left us alone, long before Uncle Peter came, didn't he, darling?
STEWART   Jane, it's not true –
JANE   You left me long before –
STEWART   I left you because of him –
JANE   I only went to him because you didn't love me, do you think I would have otherwise?
STEWART   You'd been looking at him for months.
JANE   Do you think I would have loved him?
STEWART   That's why I got out and left you to it –
JANE   You pretend you didn't leave till you left for good, but you'd been gone before that, days and days you spent away –
STEWART   Oh, don't let's have it all again.
JANE   – because you didn't love me, you never loved, you left me first, didn't he, Dad?
STEWART   Jane, we've had it all so many times.
JANE   (*Crying by now*) Didn't he, Tim? He left us, he left us first –
TIM   Don't cry! Don't you cry! I hate you! Don't cry! Don't!
STEWART   Tim –

TIM   I hate you! Ant! Ant! Ant! (*He cries*)
JANE   (*Still cries*)
STEWART   Oh, to hell with this. I'll phone you. (*He goes*)

Pause

JANE   Stewart, Stewart, wait. (*Her voice is fainter as she follows him into the house. The car starts and goes. She calls again*)
TIM   (*Still sniffs and sobs*)
G'FATHER   Come on, Tim! Let's find something to do. It's all right, they've all gone away, we're all alone now. All alone and it's getting dark. Now I know what we'll do, I'll just go to the garage, you wait there like a good boy, all by yourself, all right? You watch the sea and tell me if the lighthouse has started up yet, all right? You count how long it is between the flashes. (*He goes, leaving* TIM *looking over the rail*)
TIM   You ant you. Live by myself. I'll fly in a plane. There it is. One, two, three. You go away. Four, five. One, two. I'll fly away in a plane. Don't cry, I hate you. One two three four five.
G'FATHER   Now come on, Tim, this is what we'll do. Can you see where the ants are in the dark? You can just see, can't you? Pour a little petrol on them, that's right. Now we put the string here in the petrol and bring the end way over here so we can shelter from the blast, all right? Down we crouch, then, oh. Now we light the string, here, see, light the string. (*He strikes a match*) You take the match, you do it. That's right. Blow out the match. Now you wait, the string will burn all the way down to the enemy, see the little flame go all the way down to the ants.

The petrol explodes into flame.

TIM   (*Shrieks with laughter*)

Separated Twins

from the stage play *Blood Brothers* (1981)

by Willy Russell

This play was originally devised for performance in schools and then adapted into a West End musical. Mrs Johnston ('The Mother') is a working-class Liverpudlian. She has had seven children, has been deserted by their father, and is pregnant again. The script describes her as 'thirty, but looks sixty'. She introduces herself in a song.

Characters

THE MOTHER, Mrs Johnston
CHORUS (can be read by a single speaker)
EDWARD (EDDIE), aged seven
MICKEY, his twin brother
MRS LYONS, who has adopted Edward

THE MOTHER Once I had a husband
You know the sort of chap.
I met him at a dance and how he came on with the chat.
He said my eyes were deep blue pools
My skin as soft as snow
He told me I was sexier
Than Marilyn Monroe
And we went dancing
CHORUS Bob bob a bob bob bob a bob
CHORUS/THE MOTHER
Oh we went dancing

THE MOTHER	Then of course I found
	That I was six weeks overdue
	We got married at the registry and then we had a do.
	We all had curly salmon sandwiches
	And how the ale did flow;
	They said the bride was lovelier
	Than Marilyn Monroe
	And we went dancing
CHORUS	(*As before*) Oh we went dancing
THE MOTHER	Then the baby came along
	We called him Darren Wayne
	Then three months on I found that I was in the club again
	And though I still fancied dancing
	My husband wouldn't go
	With a wife he said
	Was twice the size
	Of Marilyn Monroe
	No more dancing
CHORUS	(*As before*) No more dancing
THE MOTHER	By the time that I was twenty-five
	I looked like forty-two
	With seven hungry mouths to feed and one more nearly due
	Me husband had walked out on me
	A month or two ago
	For a girl, they say
	Who looks a bit like Marilyn Monroe
	And they go dancing
CHORUS	(*As before*)
	Yes they go dancing
	Oh they go dancing, yes they go dancing ...

Mrs Johnston (The Mother) is very short of money and has desperate difficulties keeping her children. She works as a cleaner in the large house of Mrs Lyons, who wants to have children but cannot. Her husband does not want to adopt but wants to have his own children. As Mrs Lyons says:

> I wanted to adopt but Mr Lyons is, well ... He says he always wanted his own son, not someone else's. Myself I believe that an adopted child can become one's own.

Mrs Johnston then finds that she is pregnant with twins. She declares:

> With one more baby we could have managed. But not with two. The Welfare's already been on to me. They say I'm incapable of controlling the kids I've already got. They say I should put some of them into care.

Mrs Lyons suddenly thinks of an idea: she suggests that Mrs Johnston hand one of the babies to her at birth; they will bring them up separately; they will never see each other. Mrs Johnston does this, and Mrs Lyons is very careful that her growing son, Edward, does not meet his brother, who lives a little way away. But the boys meet.

Act 2, scene 2

EDWARD *appears. He is, at once, bright and forthcoming.*

EDDIE Hellow.
MICKEY (*Suspicious*) Hello.
EDDIE I've seen you before.
MICKEY Where?
EDDIE You were playing with some other boys near my house.
MICKEY Do you live up by the park?
EDDIE Yes. Are you going to come and play there again?
MICKEY No. I would. But I'm not allowed.
EDDIE Why?
MICKEY I don't know.

EDDIE Well, I'm not allowed to play down here actually.
MICKEY Give us a sweet.
EDDIE All right. (*He begins to pull out a large bag of sweets*)
MICKEY (*Shocked*) What?
EDDIE (*Offering the bag*) Here.
MICKEY (*Suspiciously taking one. Trying to work out the catch. EDDIE beaming brightly at him. MICKEY takes one and saves it*) Can I have another one? For our Sammy.
EDDIE Yes of course. Take as many as you want.
MICKEY (*Taking a handful*) Are you soft?
EDDIE I don't think so.
MICKEY Round here if you ask anyone for a sweet you have to ask about, about twenty-four million times you know. And you know what?
EDDIE (*Sitting beside him*) What?
MICKEY They still don't bleeding give you one. Sometimes our Sammy does but you have to be dead careful if Sammy gives you a sweet.
EDDIE Why?
MICKEY Because if Sammy gives you a sweet he's usually weed on it first.
EDDIE (*Exploding with giggles*) Oh that sounds like super fun.
MICKEY It is if you're our Sammy.
EDDIE Do you want to come and play?
MICKEY I might do. But I'm not playing now because I'm pissed off.
EDDIE (*Awed*) Pissed off! You say smashing things don't you? Pissed off. Do you know any more words like that?
MICKEY Yeh. Yeh I know loads of words like that. You know like the 'F' word.
EDDIE (*Clueless*) Pardon?
MICKEY You know, the 'F' word. (EDDIE *puzzled still,* MICKEY *checking that no one is around before whispering in* EDDIE*'s ear. The two of them immediately wriggling and giggling with glee*)

EDDIE What does it mean?
MICKEY I don't know. It sounds good though, doesn't it?
EDDIE Fantastic. When I get home I shall look it up in the dictionary.
MICKEY In the what?
EDDIE In the dictionary. Don't you know what a dictionary is?
MICKEY 'Course I do. It's a thingy isn't it?
EDDIE A book which tells you the meaning of words.
MICKEY Yeh. I know.
EDDIE Will you be my best friend?
MICKEY Yeh. Yeh if you want.
EDDIE And I shall be your best friend. What's your name?
MICKEY Michael Johnston. But everyone calls me Mickey. What's yours?
EDDIE Edward.
MICKEY And they call you Eddie?
EDDIE No!
MICKEY Well I will.
EDDIE Will you?
MICKEY Yeh. How old are you, Eddie?
EDDIE Seven.
MICKEY I'm older than you. I'm nearly eight.
EDDIE Well I'm nearly eight really.
MICKEY When's your birthday?
EDDIE December the twelfth.
MICKEY So is mine.
EDDIE Is it really?
MICKEY Hey, we were born on the same day. That means we can be blood brothers. Do you want to be my blood brother, Eddie?
EDDIE What do I have to do?
MICKEY It hurts you know. (MICKEY *taking out his penknife, cuts his hand*) Now give us your hand. (*Does the same to* EDDIE *and then clamps the hands together*) See this means

that we're blood brothers and that we always have to stand by each other. Now, you have to say after me: 'I will always defend my brother ...'

EDDIE   I will always defend my brother ...
THE MOTHER   (*Off*) Mickey ... Mickey ...
EDDIE   Is that your mummy?

THE MOTHER *appearing*

MICKEY   Mam, this is my brother.
THE MOTHER   (*Stunned*) What?
MICKEY   My blood brother, Eddie.
THE MOTHER   Eddie. Eddie who?
EDDIE   Edward Lyons, Mrs Johnston.

THE MOTHER *stares at him.*

MICKEY   Eddie's my best friend now, Mam. He lives up by the park but ...
THE MOTHER   Mickey, get in the house ...
MICKEY   What?
THE MOTHER   (*Threatening*) Get in!

The bright and eager smile disappears from EDDIE*'s face.*

MICKEY   But I've only ...
THE MOTHER   Get!
MICKEY   (*Going, almost crying*) I haven't done nothing. I'll see you, Eddie.
EDDIE   Erm. Erm have I done something, Mrs Johnston?
THE MOTHER   Does your mother know you're down here?
  (EDDIE *shaking his head*) What would she say if she knew?
EDDIE   I ... I think she'd be angry.
THE MOTHER   So don't you think you'd better go home before she finds out?
EDDIE   I suppose so.
THE MOTHER   Go on then.

He turns to go and then stops.

EDDIE Could I ... would it be all right if I came to play with Mickey on another day? Or perhaps he could come and play at my house ...

HE MOTHER Don't you ever come around here again. Ever.

EDDIE But ...

HE MOTHER Ever! Now go on ... beat it ... go on, go home before the bogey man gets you.

She watches as he leaves and stands, staring after him.

Act 2, scene 3

She watches as the scene forms in which we see EDDIE *at home, leafing through a dictionary.* MRS LYONS *entering and kissing him on the head.* EDDIE *turning and smiling at her.*

EDDIE Mum ... Mummy ...

THE MOTHER *turns and leaves.*

EDDIE Mum how do you spell 'bogey man'?

MRS LYONS (*Laughing*) Wherever did you hear such a word?

EDDIE I erm ... I'm trying to look it up ... what is a bogey man?

MRS LYONS (*Laughing*) Edward ... there's no such thing. It's erm, it's just an idea of something bad. It's a, a superstition. The sort of thing a silly mother would say to her children 'the bogey man will get you'.

EDDIE Will he get me?

MRS LYONS Edward ... I've told you, there's no such thing.

There is a loud knocking at the door. MRS LYONS *goes off to answer the door.*

MICKEY (*Off*) Does Eddie live here?

MRS LYONS Pardon?
MICKEY Does he? Is he coming out to play?
EDDIE (*Looking up. Delighted*) Mickey!

MRS LYONS *and* MICKEY *entering*.

MICKEY Hiya, Eddie. Look, I've got our Sammy's catapult. You coming out eh?
EDDIE (*Taking the catapult and trying a practice shot*) Ogh ... Isn't Mickey fantastic, Mum?
MRS LYONS Do you go to the same school as Edward?
MICKEY No.
EDDIE Mickey says smashing things. We're blood brothers, aren't we, Mickey?
MICKEY Yeh. We were born on the same day.
EDDIE Come on Mickey ... Let's go ... !
MRS LYONS Edward! Edward it's time for bed.
EDDIE Mummy, it's not.
MRS LYONS (*Ushering* MICKEY *out*) I'm very sorry but it's Edward's bedtime.
EDDIE Mummy! Mummy, it's early! (MRS LYONS *returning after having shown* MICKEY *the door*) Mummy!
MRS LYONS Edward. Where did you meet that boy?
EDDIE (*Petulant*) At his house.
MRS LYONS His second name ... his second name is Johnston ... isn't it Edward?
EDDIE Yes! And I think you're very mean!
MRS LYONS I've told you never to go where that boy lives.
EDDIE But why?
MRS LYONS Because ... because you're not the same as him. You're not! Do you understand?
EDDIE No! No I don't understand ... And I hate you!

Instinctively she whacks him across the head but is immediately appalled.

MRS LYONS Edward, Edward ... (*Pulling him to her, cradling him*)

Edward you must understand, it's for your own good. It's only because I love you, Edward.

EDDIE (*Breaking away. Complete rage*) You don't! If you loved me you'd let me go out with Mickey because he's my best friend. I like him more than you.

MRS LYONS Edward! Edward, don't say that.

EDDIE Well. Well it's true. I know what you are!

MRS LYONS What?

EDDIE You're a ... you're a fuckoff!

MRS LYONS lunges across the room, grabs him by the wrist and shakes the terrified child, screaming at him.

MRS LYONS You see ... you see why I don't want you mixing with boys like that. Filth; you learn filth and you behave like this ... like a horrible little boy ... like them, like them ... you're behaving like them and I won't have it, do you understand? (*She is slightly out of control, shaking him. He stares in terror*) You're my son, mine ... you won't behave like them, like him ... you won't ... you won't ... (*She suddenly sees the fear in his face. Almost crying she gently pulls him to her and cradles him*) Oh my son ... my son ...

The scene freezes.

Who Is the True Mother?

from the stage play
The Caucasian Chalk Circle   (1954)

by Bertolt Brecht

(translated by James and Tanya Stern and W. H. Auden)

An ancient tale set in China is used to make a modern point about true motherhood. At a time of battle and revolt, the rich and powerful Governor Abashvili and his wife have a baby. When the opposing armies attack, the governor's wife is too worried about her rich clothes to make proper arrangements for the care of the child. Baby Michael is abandoned. A servant girl, Grusha, has recently fallen in love with a young soldier, Simon. The extract begins with her last words to him as he has to leave with the army.

Characters

GRUSHA VACHNADZE, a kitchenmaid in the royal palace
SIMON CHACHAVA, a soldier
THE NURSE
THE FAT WOMAN, Nina
THE STABLEMAN
THE THIRD WOMAN
THE COOK
THE FAT PRINCE
THE SINGER, a narrator
THE CORPORAL
AZDAK, village recorder acting as Judge
THE FIRST LAWYER, Illo Shuboladze
THE GOVERNOR'S WIFE, Natella Abashvili

WHO IS THE TRUE MOTHER?

THE SECOND LAWYER, Sandro Obolodze
SHAUVA, an officer
THE OLD WOMAN
THE OLD MAN

GRUSHA Simon Chachava, I shall wait for you.
Go calmly into battle, soldier
The bloody battle, the bitter battle
From which not everyone returns.
When you return I will be there.
I will be waiting for you under the green elm
I will be waiting for you under the bare elm
I will wait until the last soldier has returned
And even longer.
When you return from the battle
No boots will lie before the door
The pillow beside mine will be empty
My mouth will be unkissed.
When you return, when you return
You will be able to say: all is as it was.

SIMON I thank you, Grusha Vachnadze, and farewell!

He bows low before her; she bows low before him. Then she runs off without looking round.

As the chaos rises, the governor's wife makes her escape.

NURSE (*Entering through the gateway with her mistress's slippers*) Madam!
FAT WOMAN She's gone.
NURSE And the child. (*She rushes to the child, and picks it up*) They left it behind, those brutes! (*She hands the child to* GRUSHA) Hold it for a moment. (*Deceitfully*) I'm going to look for the carriage.

She runs off, following the GOVERNOR'S WIFE.

GRUSHA What have they done to the Governor?
STABLEMAN (*Drawing his index finger across his throat*) Fft.
FAT WOMAN (*Seeing the gesture, becomes hysterical*) Oh God! Oh God! Oh God! Our master Georgi Abashvili! At morning Mass he was a picture of health! And now! Oh, take me away! We're all lost! We must die in sin! Like our master, Georgi Abashvili!
3RD WOMAN (*Trying to calm her*) Calm down, Nina. You'll get away. You've done no one any harm.
FAT WOMAN (*Being led out*) Oh God! Oh God! Oh God! Let's all get out before they come! Before they come!
3RD WOMAN Nina takes it to heart more than the mistress. People like that get others even to do their *weeping* for them! (*Seeing the child in* GRUSHA*'s arms*) The child! What are you doing with it?
GRUSHA It's been left behind.
3RD WOMAN She just left it? Michael, who was never allowed to be in a draught!

The servants gather round the child.

GRUSHA He's waking up.
STABLEMAN Better put him down, I tell you. I'd rather not think what'd happen to the person seen with that child. I'll get our things. You wait here.

Exit into the palace.

COOK He's right. Once they begin, they'll slaughter whole families. I'll go and fetch my belongings.

All go except the COOK, *the* 3RD WOMAN *and* GRUSHA *with the child in her arms.*

3RD WOMAN Didn't you hear? Better put him down!
GRUSHA The nurse asked me to hold him for a moment.

WHO IS THE TRUE MOTHER?

COOK That one won't come back, you silly!

3RD WOMAN Keep your hands off him.

COOK They'll be more after him than after his mother. He's the heir. Grusha, you're a good soul. But you know you're not too bright. I tell you, if he had the plague it couldn't be worse. Better see to it that you get away.

The STABLEMAN has come back carrying bundles which he distributes among the women. They all prepare to leave except GRUSHA.

GRUSHA (*Stubbornly*) He hasn't got the plague. He looks at you like a human being.

COOK Then don't you look back. You're just the kind of fool who always gets put upon. If someone says to you: Run and get the lettuce, you have the longest legs! – you run. We're taking the ox-cart, you can have a lift if you hurry. Jesus, by now the whole neighbourhood must be in flames!

3RD WOMAN Haven't you packed anything yet? There isn't much time, you know. The Ironshirts will soon be here from the barracks.

Exit both women and the STABLEMAN.

GRUSHA I'm coming.

GRUSHA lays the child down, looks at it for a moment, then takes clothes from the trunks lying about and covers the sleeping child. Then she runs into the palace to get her things. Sounds of horses' hoofs and of women screaming. Enter the FAT PRINCE with drunken Ironshirts. One of them carries the head of the Governor on a lance.

FAT PRINCE Put it here. Right in the middle! (*One Ironshirt climbs on to the back of another, takes the head and holds it over the gateway*) That's not the middle. Further to the right. Good. What I do, my friends, I do well. (*While an*

Ironshirt with hammer and nail fastens the head by its hair) This morning at the church door I said to Georgi Abashvili: 'I love a clear sky.' Actually, what I prefer is lightning from a clear sky. Oh, yes. But it's a pity they took the brat away. I need him. Badly. Search the whole of Grusinia for him! 1000 piastres reward!

As GRUSHA *enters cautiously through the doorway, the* FAT PRINCE *and the Ironshirts leave. Trampling of horses' hoofs again. Carrying a bundle,* GRUSHA *walks towards the gateway. At the last moment, she turns to see if the child is still there. Promptly the* SINGER *begins to sing. She stands rooted to the spot.*

SINGER As she was standing between courtyard and gate, she heard
Or thought she heard, a low voice. The child
Called to her, not whining but calling quite sensibly
At least so it seemed to her: 'Woman,' it said, 'Help me.'
Went on calling not whining but calling quite sensibly:
'Don't you know, woman, that she who does not listen to a cry for help
But passes by shutting her ears, will never hear
The gentle call of a lover
Nor the blackbird at dawn, nor the happy
Sigh of the exhausted grape-picker at the sound of the Angelus.
Hearing this

GRUSHA *walks a few steps towards the child and bends over it.*

            she went back to the child
Just for one more look, just to sit with it

For a moment or two till someone should come
Its mother, perhaps, or someone else –

She sits down opposite the child, and leans against a trunk.

Just for a moment before she left, for now the
 danger was too great
The city full of flame and grief.

The light grows dimmer as though evening and night were falling, GRUSHA *has gone into the palace and fetched a lamp and some milk, which she gives the child to drink.*

SINGER (*Loudly*)
Terrible is the temptation to do good!

GRUSHA *now settles down to keep watch over the child through the night. Once, she lights a small lamp to look at it. Once, she tucks it in with a brocade coat. Now and again she listens and looks up to see if someone is coming.*

For a long time she sat with the child.
Evening came, night came, dawn came.
Too long she sat, too long she watched
The soft breathing, the little fists
Till towards morning the temptation grew too
 strong.
She rose, she leaned over, she sighed, she lifted the
 child
She carried it off.

She does what the SINGER *says as he describes it.*

Like booty she took it for herself
Like a thief she sneaked away.

Grusha struggles to look after the baby, but is pursued by the soldiers who are searching for him. A corporal from the prince's Ironshirts sees the child and tries to take it. She risks her life saving the child and escaping with it, and then comes to feel for the child she is caring for as a mother.

CORPORAL Well, there's the child I wanted to have from you. (*He walks towards the crib*)

GRUSHA Officer, it's mine. It's not the one you're after.

CORPORAL I'll just have a look at it. (*He bends over the crib.* GRUSHA *looks round in despair*)

GRUSHA It's mine! It's mine!

CORPORAL Nice linen!

> GRUSHA *jumps at him to pull him away. He throws her off and again bends over the crib. Looking round in despair, she suddenly sees a big log of wood, seizes it in panic, and hits the* CORPORAL *over the head from behind. She quickly picks up the child and dashes off.*

SINGER After her escape from the Ironshirts
After twenty-two days of wandering
At the foot of the Janga-Tau glacier
From this moment Grusha Vachnadze decided to be the child's mother.
The helpless girl
Became the mother of the helpless child.

> GRUSHA *squats over a half-frozen stream to ladle some water in her hand for the child.*

GRUSHA Nobody wants to take you
So I shall have to take you
There is no one else but me, my dear
On this black day in a meagre year
Who will not forsake you.
Since I've carried you too long
And with sore feet
Since the milk was too dear
I grew fond of you.

WHO IS THE TRUE MOTHER?

(I wouldn't be without you any more.)
I'll throw your fine little shirt away
And wrap you in rags
I'll wash you and christen you
With glacier water.
(You'll have to bear it.)

She has taken off the child's fine linen and wrapped it in a rag.

Grusha is persuaded to marry a very sick man to give her and the baby some security. Then the war is over, and she is captured. Simon has returned. The governor is dead, and the governor's wife is seeking her child. She takes Grusha to court to get the child back. As the dead governor's land and riches have been left to his baby son, the governor's wife needs the child for its wealth. A strange man has been made judge: Azdak. He hears the argument between Grusha and the governor's wife. Grusha wants to bring up the child, but she can't if the governor's wife is given it. She wants to marry Simon, but she can't because of her arranged marriage. The very odd judge hears the case. He is willing to take bribes, but underneath his oddness he has a real human sense.

LAWYERS (*Approaching* AZDAK, *who stands up expectantly*) An absolutely ridiculous case, Your Worship. The accused has abducted the child and refuses to hand it over.

AZDAK (*Stretching out his hand, and glancing at* GRUSHA) A most attractive person. (*He receives more money*) I open the proceedings and demand the absolute truth. (*To* GRUSHA) Especially from you.

1ST LAWYER High Court of Justice! Blood, as the saying goes, is thicker than water. This old proverb ...

AZDAK The Court wants to know the lawyer's fee.

1ST LAWYER (*Surprised*) I beg your pardon? (AZDAK *rubs his thumb and index finger*) Oh, I see. 500 piastres, Your Worship, is the answer to the Court's somewhat unusual question.

AZDAK Did you hear? The question is unusual. I ask it because I listen to you in a quite different way if I know you are good.

1ST LAWYER (*Bowing*) Thank you, Your Worship. High Court of Justice! Of all bonds the bonds of blood are the strongest. Mother and child – is there a more intimate relationship? Can one tear a child from its mother? High Court of Justice! She has conceived it in the holy ecstasies of love. She has carried it in her womb. She has fed it with her blood. She has borne it with pain. High Court of Justice! It has been observed, Your Worship, how even the wild tigress, robbed of her young, roams restless through the mountains, reduced to a shadow. Nature herself ...

AZDAK (*Interrupting, to* GRUSHA) What's your answer to all this and anything else the lawyer might have to say?

GRUSHA He's mine.

AZDAK Is that all? I hope you can prove it. In any case, I advise you to tell me why you think the child should be given to you.

GRUSHA I've brought him up 'according to my best knowledge and conscience'. I always found him something to eat. Most of the time he had a roof over his head. And I went to all sorts of trouble for him. I had expenses, too. I didn't think of my own comfort. I brought up the child to be friendly with everyone. And from the beginning I taught him to work as well as he could. But he's still very small.

1ST LAWYER Your Worship, it is significant that the person herself doesn't claim any bond of blood between herself and this child.

AZDAK The Court takes note.

1ST LAWYER Thank you, Your Worship. Please permit a woman who has suffered much – who has already lost her husband and now also has to fear the loss of her child – to address a few words to you. Her Highness, Natella Abashvili ...

GOV'S WIFE (*Quietly*) A most cruel fate, sir, forces me to ask you to return my beloved child. It's not for me to describe to you the tortures of a bereaved mother's soul, the anxiety, the sleepless nights, the ...

2ND LAWYER (*Exploding*) It's outrageous the way this woman is treated. She's not allowed to enter her husband's palace. The revenue of her estates is blocked. She is told cold-bloodedly that it's tied to the heir. She can't do anything without the child. She can't even pay her lawyers. (*To the* 1ST LAWYER *who, desperate about this outburst, makes frantic gestures to stop him speaking*) Dear Illo Shuboladze, why shouldn't it be divulged now that it's the Abashvili estates that are at stake?

1ST LAWYER Please, Honoured Sandro Obolodze! We had agreed ... (*To* AZDAK) Of course it is correct that the trial will also decide whether our noble client will obtain the right to dispose of the large Abashvili estates. I say 'also' on purpose, because in the foreground stands the human tragedy of a mother, as Natella Abashvili has rightly explained at the beginning of her moving statement. Even if Michael Abashvili were *not* the heir to the estates, he would still be the dearly beloved child of my client.

AZDAK Stop! The Court is touched by the mention of the estates. It's a proof of human feeling.

2ND LAWYER Thanks, Your Worship. Dear Illo Shuboladze, in any case we can prove that the person who took possession of the child is not the child's mother. Permit me to lay before the Court the bare facts. By an unfortunate chain of circumstances, the child, Michael Abashvili, was left behind while his mother was making her escape. Grusha, the Palace kitchenmaid, was present on this Easter Sunday and was observed busying herself with the child …

COOK All her mistress was thinking about was what kind of dresses she would take along.

2ND LAWYER (*Unmoved*) Almost a year later Grusha turned up in a mountain village with a child, and there entered into matrimony with …

AZDAK How did you get into that mountain village?

GRUSHA On foot, Your Worship. And he was mine.

SIMON I am the father, Your Worship.

COOK I had him in my care for five piastres, Your Worship.

2ND LAWYER This man is engaged to Grusha, High Court of Justice, and for this reason his testimony is not reliable.

AZDAK Are you the man she married in the mountain village?

SIMON No, Your Worship, she married a peasant.

AZDAK (*Winking at* GRUSHA) Why? (*Pointing at* SIMON) Isn't he any good in bed? Tell the truth.

GRUSHA We didn't get that far. I married because of the child, so that he should have a roof over his head. (*Pointing at* SIMON) He was in the war, Your Worship.

AZDAK And now he wants you again, eh?

SIMON I want to state in evidence …

GRUSHA (*Angrily*) I am no longer free, Your Worship.

AZDAK And the child, you claim, is the result of whoring? (GRUSHA *does not answer*) I'm going to ask you a question: What kind of child is it? Is it one of those ragged street-urchins? Or is it a child from a well-to-do family?

WHO IS THE TRUE MOTHER?

GRUSHA (*Angrily*) It's an ordinary child.

AZDAK I mean, did he have fine features from the beginning?

GRUSHA He had a nose in his face.

AZDAK He had a nose in his face. I consider that answer of yours to be important. They say of me that once, before passing judgment, I went out and sniffed at a rosebush. Tricks of this kind are necessary nowadays. I'll cut things short now, and listen no longer to your lies. (*To* GRUSHA) Especially yours. (*To the group of defendants*) I can imagine what you've cooked up between you to cheat me. I know you. You're swindlers.

GRUSHA (*Suddenly*) I can quite understand your wanting to cut it short, having seen what you received!

AZDAK Shut up! Did I receive anything from you?

GRUSHA (*While the cook tries to restrain her*) Because I haven't got anything.

AZDAK Quite true. I never get a thing from starvelings. I might just as well starve myself. You want justice, but do you want to pay for it? When you go to the butcher you know you have to pay. But to the Judge you go as though to a funeral supper.

SIMON (*Loudly*) 'When the horse was shod, the horsefly stretched out its leg', as the saying is.

AZDAK (*Eagerly accepting the challenge*) 'Better a treasure in the sewer than a stone in the mountain stream.'

SIMON '"A fine day. Let's go fishing," said the angler to the worm.'

AZDAK '"I'm my own master," said the servant, and cut off his foot.'

SIMON '"I love you like a father," said the Czar to the peasant, and had the Czarevitch's head chopped off.'

AZDAK 'The fool's worst enemy is himself.'

SIMON But 'a fart has no nose'.

AZDAK Fined ten piastres for indecent language in Court. That'll teach you what Justice is.

GRUSHA That's a fine kind of Justice. You jump on us because we don't talk so refined as that lot with their lawyers.

AZDAK Exactly. The likes of you are too stupid. It's only right that you should get it in the neck.

GRUSHA Because you want to pass the child on to her. She who is too refined even to know how to change its nappies! You don't know any more about Justice than I do, that's clear.

AZDAK There's something in that. I'm an ignorant man. I haven't even a decent pair of trousers under my robe. See for yourself. With me, everything goes on food and drink. I was educated in a convent school. Come to think of it, I'll fine you ten piastres, too. For contempt of Court. What's more, you're a very silly girl to turn me against you, instead of making eyes at me and wagging your backside a bit to keep me in a good temper. Twenty piastres!

GRUSHA Even if it were thirty, I'd tell you what I think of your justice, you drunken onion! How dare you talk to me as though you were the cracked Isaiah on the church window! When they pulled you out of your mother, it wasn't planned that you'd rap her over the knuckles for pinching a little bowl of corn from somewhere! Aren't you ashamed of yourself when you see how afraid I am of you? But you've let yourself become their servant. So that their houses are not taken away, because they've stolen them. Since when do houses belong to bed-bugs? But you're on the look-out, otherwise they couldn't drag our men into their wars. You bribe-taker!

AZDAK gets up. He begins to beam. With a little hammer he knocks on the table half-heartedly as if to get silence. But as GRUSHA's *scolding continues, he only beats time with it.*

I've no respect for you. No more than for a thief or a murderer with a knife, who does what he wants. You can take the child away from me, a hundred against one, but I tell you one thing: for a profession like yours, they ought to choose only bloodsuckers and men who rape children. As a punishment. To make them sit in judgment over their fellow men, which is worse than swinging from the gallows.

AZDAK (*Sitting down*) Now it will be thirty! And I won't go on brawling with you as though we were in a tavern. What would happen to my dignity as a Judge? I've lost all interest in your case. Where's the couple who wanted a divorce? (*To* SHAUVA) Bring them in. This case is adjourned for fifteen minutes.

1ST LAWYER (*To the* GOVERNOR'S WIFE) Without producing any more evidence, Madam, we have the verdict in the bag.

COOK (*To* GRUSHA) You've gone and spoiled your chances with him. You won't get the child now.

Enter a very old couple.

GOV'S WIFE Shalva, my smelling salts!
AZDAK I receive. (*The old couple do not understand*) I hear you want to be divorced. How long have you been living together?
OLD WOMAN Forty years, Your Worship.
AZDAK And why d'you want a divorce?
OLD MAN We don't like each other, Your Worship.
AZDAK Since when?
OLD WOMAN Oh, from the very beginning, Your Worship.
AZDAK I'll consider your case and deliver my verdict when I'm finished with the other one. (SHAUVA *leads them*

into the background) I need the child. (*He beckons* GRUSHA *towards him and bends not unkindly towards her*) I've noticed that you have a soft spot for justice. I don't believe he's your child, but if he were yours, woman, wouldn't you want him to be rich? You'd only have to say he isn't yours and at once he'd have a palace, scores of horses in his stable, scores of beggars on his doorstep, scores of soldiers in his service, and scores of petitioners in his courtyard. Now, what d'you say? Don't you want him to be rich?

GRUSHA *is silent*.

SINGER Listen now to what the angry girl thought, but didn't say:

He sings.

He who wears the shoes of gold
Tramples on the weak and old
Does evil all day long
And mocks at wrong.

O to carry as one's own
Heavy is the heart of stone.
The power to do ill
Wears out the will.

Hunger he will dread
Not those who go unfed:
Fear the fall of night
But not the light.

AZDAK I think I understand you, woman.
GRUSHA I won't give him away. I've brought him up, and he knows me.

Enter SHAUVA *with the child.*

WHO IS THE TRUE MOTHER?

GOV'S WIFE It's in rags!

GRUSHA That's not true. I wasn't given the time to put on his good shirt.

GOV'S WIFE It's been in a pigsty.

GRUSHA (*Furious*) I'm no pig, but there are others who are. Where did you leave your child?

GOV'S WIFE I'll let you have it, you vulgar person. (*She is about to throw herself on* GRUSHA, *but is restrained by her lawyers*) She's a criminal! She must be whipped!

2ND LAWYER (*Holding his hand over her mouth*) Most gracious Natella Abashvili, you promised ... Your Worship, the plaintiff's nerves ...

AZDAK Plaintiff and defendant! The Court has listened to your case, and has come to no decision as to who the real mother of this child is. I as Judge have the duty of choosing a mother for the child. I'll make a test. Shauva, get a piece of chalk and draw a circle on the floor. (SHAUVA *does so*) Now place the child in the centre. (SHAUVA *puts* MICHAEL, *who smiles at* GRUSHA, *in the centre of the circle*) Stand near the circle, both of you. (*The* GOVERNOR'S WIFE *and* GRUSHA *step up to the circle*) Now each of you take the child by a hand. The true mother is she who has the strength to pull the child out of the circle, towards herself.

2ND LAWYER (*Quickly*) High Court of Justice, I protest! I object that the fate of the great Abashvili estates, which are bound up with the child as the heir, should be made dependent on such a doubtful wrestling match. Moreover, my client does not command the same physical strength as this person, who is accustomed to physical work.

AZDAK She looks pretty well fed to me. Pull!

The GOVERNOR'S WIFE *pulls the child out of the circle to her side.* GRUSHA *has let it go and stands aghast.*

1ST LAWYER (*Congratulating the* GOVERNOR'S WIFE) What did I say! The bonds of blood!

AZDAK (*To* GRUSHA) What's the matter with you? You didn't pull!

GRUSHA I didn't hold on to him. (*She runs to* AZDAK) Your Worship, I take back everything I said against you. I ask your forgiveness. If I could just keep him until he can speak properly. He knows only a few words.

AZDAK Don't influence the Court! I bet you know only twenty yourself. All right, I'll do the test once more, to make certain.

The two women take up positions again.

AZDAK Pull!

Again GRUSHA *lets go of the child.*

GRUSHA (*In despair*) I've brought him up! Am I to tear him to pieces? I can't do it!

AZDAK (*Rising*) And in this manner the Court has established the true mother. (*To* GRUSHA) Take your child and be off with it. I advise you not to stay in town with him. (*To the* GOVERNOR'S WIFE) And you disappear before I fine you for fraud. Your estates fall to the city. A playground for children will be made out of them. They need one, and I have decided it shall be called after me – The Garden of Azdak.

The GOVERNOR'S WIFE *has fainted and is carried out by the Adjutant. Her* LAWYERS *have preceded her.* GRUSHA *stands motionless.* SHAUVA *leads the child towards her.*

AZDAK Now I'll take off this Judge's robe – it has become too hot for me. I'm not cut out for a hero. But I invite you all to a little farewell dance, outside on the meadow. Oh, I had almost forgotten something in my excitement. I haven't signed the decree for divorce.

WHO IS THE TRUE MOTHER?

Using the Judge's seat as a table, he writes something on a piece of paper and prepares to leave. Dance music has started.

SHAUVA (*Having read what is on the paper*) But that's not right. You haven't divorced the old couple. You've divorced Grusha from her husband.

AZDAK Have I divorced the wrong ones? I'm sorry, but it'll have to stand. I never retract anything. If I did, there'd be no law and order. (*To the old couple*) Instead, I'll invite you to my feast. You won't mind dancing with each other. (*To* GRUSHA *and* SIMON) I've still got 40 piastres coming from you.

SIMON (*Pulling out his purse*) That's cheap, Your Worship. And many thanks.

AZDAK (*Pocketing the money*) I'll need it.

GRUSHA So we'd better leave town tonight, eh, Michael? (*About to take the child on her back. To* SIMON) You like him?

SIMON (*Taking the child on his back*) With my respects, I like him.

GRUSHA And now I can tell you: I took him because on that Easter Sunday I got engaged to you. And so it is a child of love. Michael, let's dance.

She dances with MICHAEL. SIMON *dances with the* COOK. *The old couple dance with each other.* AZDAK *stands lost in thought. The dancers soon hide him from view. Occasionally he is seen again, but less and less as more couples enter and join the dance.*

SINGER And after this evening Azdak disappeared and was never seen again.
But the people of Grusinia did not forget him and often remembered
His time of Judgment as a brief
Golden Age that was almost just.

The dancing couples dance out. AZDAK *has disappeared.*

But you, who have listened to the story of the Chalk Circle
Take note of the meaning of the ancient song:
That what there is shall belong to those who are good for it, thus
The children to the maternal, that they thrive;
The carriages to good drivers, that they are driven well;
And the valley to the waterers, that it shall bear fruit.

Death in the Barn

from the television play
Blue Remembered Hills   (1979)

by Dennis Potter

It is a summer afternoon during the Second World War, in the West Country. There is a stretch of common, a wood, and a field with an old barn in it. Nearby there is an Italian prisoner-of-war camp. The seven characters in the play are all seven-year-old children: five boys and two girls. Audrey is aggressive and disgruntled and takes it out on the boys. She is plain, and jealous of Angela's prettiness. Angela has a china doll called Dinah, whom she pushes around in a battered old pram. Burly Peter is the bully. Raymond stutters. Donald, whose nick-name is Donald Duck, is a splay-footed, anaemic-looking boy with scabs around his mouth; he wears no socks. His father is missing in the war and his mother abuses him. The children taunt him.

Donald has been playing 'house' with the two girls in the barn. They leave him there and meet up with the other boys. Peter and John have a fight. John wins and Peter rushes away, crying, and joins Donald in the barn. Suddenly the siren sounds from the prisoner-of-war camp. A prisoner has escaped. Willie, John, Raymond, Angela and Audrey are frightened and rush to take cover in a hollow among the trees, leaving the pram and doll behind. (The title of the play, and the verse at the end, comes from a poem by A. E. Housman.)

Characters

JOHN
ANGELA
WILLIE
AUDREY
RAYMOND
PETER
DONALD

Scene 16

The hollow. The five plunge for safety into a natural, grassy, scooped-out hollow in the midst of the trees. They huddle together, breathless and scared.

JOHN   Him won't find us down in here.
ANGELA   You sure?
JOHN   Ne-ver. 'Course him won't.
WILLIE   We didn't stand a chance out there on the path.
JOHN   (*Unsure*) This is nice and safe. Ennit?
AUDREY   What did you hear, Raymond?
RAYMOND   Him!
JOHN   Did – did you *see* him?
RAYMOND   I d-du-don't know.
ANGELA   I wanna go home.
JOHN   We'll have to stay here a bit.
WILLIE   F'r how long, though?
RAYMOND   (*Whispering*) Till d-dark – shall us?
JOHN   They'll have the guards out after him. They'll soon catch him.
AUDREY   What'll they do to him?
JOHN   Shoot him.
AUDREY   Good job.
WILLIE   Where's the pram?

ANGELA Oh. Oh. The pram! And Dinah! (*A cry*) Poor little Dinah ...

JOHN It won't hurt where it is.

ANGELA (*Wailing*) But her'll be fright-ened!

WILLIE Hold your hosses!

But she is sobbing.

JOHN Oh we'll go and get the pram. In a minute.

WILLIE Who will?

JOHN (*Licking his lips*) All of us. It'll be all right if'n we stick together. Eh?

AUDREY (*Belligerently*) Never mind the pram!

WILLIE How long we going to stay here, that's what I wanna know.

RAYMOND (*Whispering*) Must be d-du-dinner time.

WILLIE Have a look over the top, John.

JOHN (*Alarmed*) What?

WILLIE See if there's anybody moving about up there.

JOHN In a minute.

JOHN *sees* AUDREY *looking at him, and lowers his eyes.*

AUDREY You're not frightened. Are you?

JOHN 'Course not!

AUDREY Wallace Wilson 'ood go up and have a look.

JOHN In a minute, I said. Shut your mouth, Audrey.

AUDREY Oy – and *Peter* would an' all.

JOHN (*Muttering*) Shut your cakehole.

RAYMOND L-Lul-Listen!!

RAYMOND's *way of saying this is, again, of such chilling urgency that the others freeze in sheer terror. A trembling pause. Woodland sounds. Wood pigeons coo-coo.*

WILLIE (*Whispering*) Raymond? What is it?

Eyes wide, RAYMOND *clutches at the nearest arm.*

RAYMOND (*Desperately*) Hark!

Sure enough – the sound of someone running – crashing heavily through the woodland undergrowth. The five huddle closer in desperation, whimpering. A figure breaks to the top of the hollow, socks down to the ankles, bootlace undone. It is PETER.

PETER   What you doing down in there?
JOHN   Peter! (*Shamefaced*) We thought ...
AUDREY We thought you was that Wop.
PETER   (*Sniggering*) Me? That's a good 'un!
WILLIE Didn't you hear that siren thing?

PETER *is clambering down.*

PETER   Hear it? 'Course I heard it. I byun't deaf, be I? I was looking for tha'.
JOHN   What for?

PETER *looks at him.*

PETER   (*Pleased*) Frightened – was you?
JOHN   Me? 'Course I warn't.
AUDREY (*Hotly*) Yes you was! Yes him was! We been bloody crying and all down in here.
JOHN   *You* have, you mean.
PETER   Donald Duck is trembling like a jelly.
WILLIE Where is he?
PETER   The barn. Him oodn't leave. Come th'on, I said. Let's go and catch the Itie. No, him oodn't. Went back and hid in the corner.
JOHN   The sissy.
ANGELA And you be, John.
AUDREY You done the same!
JOHN   (*Stung*) That's 'cos we had you girls along, ennit? Ennit Willie? Ennit Raymond? We boys wasn't frightened, was us?

WILLIE　No!
RAYMOND　'C-cu-course not.
AUDREY　(*Jabbing her finger*) You wouldn't even have a peep, John.
ANGELA　*And* you made me leave my pram!
PETER　(*Pleased*) 'S that right?
JOHN　(*Annoyed*) I got to look a'ter 'em, enn I! This 'ere I-talian or Wop or whatever he calls hisself, might have a knife. Have you thought of that?
PETER　Ne-ver! (*But a flicker of anxiety crosses his face*)
RAYMOND　No, that's right, m-mum-mind.
JOHN　And what if him's out for blood?
WILLIE　*English* blood.

PETER *gapes at them.*

PETER　I hadn't thought of that. Him could have *got* I!
WILLIE　Stuck a knife in you.
PETER　(*Looking about*) Him won't never find us in these here woods. Will he?
JOHN　He killed two or dree guards to get out of the camp. Slit their throats.
AUDREY　(*Half-excited*) Did he?

ANGELA *wails.*

WILLIE　(*Frowning*) How do you know, John?
JOHN　That's what I heard, any road.
PETER　By Gar!
WILLIE　But you been with us all the time! You ant bin out of our sight, John.
AUDREY　You been with us all the time!
JOHN　No I ant.
AUDREY　Yes you bloody have!
JOHN　Even if I have, it's obvious, ennit?
PETER　Is it?

JOHN They don't just open the gate and let a prisoner of war out – now do 'um?
WILLIE No. 'Course not.
JOHN Him'd have to kill – oodn't he?
PETER That's right. That's it. You have got it!
RAYMOND (*Worried*) L-lul-let's go home.
JOHN Nobody's stopping you.

RAYMOND *looks at the others.*

RAYMOND Ent you c-cu-coming –?
WILLIE Shall us?
ANGELA Yes!
JOHN Nobody's stopping you.

PETER *looks at* JOHN, *and decides to line up with him.*

PETER Nobody's stopping you!
ANGELA (*Tearfully*) What about my poor little Dinah? Her'll cry and cry and cry.
WILLIE Well, I'm not going out there on me own.
RAYMOND N-nun-nor me.
AUDREY Yes, but what about her bloody doll?
ANGELA Stop cussing.
JOHN Shall we go and get'm, Peter?
PETER What? Me and you?
JOHN We be the best two.
ANGELA You can't leave us! You can't go on your own!
AUDREY Somebody's got to go.
WILLIE (*Nervously*) You won't be long, though? You *will* come back?
RAYMOND P-Pup-Please hurry up.
JOHN Just keep your heads down.
PETER And don't move.
JOHN Don't make a sound.
PETER Good job you got us, I reckon Number Two and Number Three.

JOHN *looks at him.*

JOHN Which is Number Two?

Slight, sad pause.

PETER You be.
JOHN Peter's right. It's a good job you got us. (*Warmly*) Come on Peter, old pal—
PETER (*Anxiously*) You sure?
JOHN We gotta take a chance.
PETER Oy. Come on then.
JOHN Wait here, you lot. (*To* PETER) Come on.

But they haven't moved.

PETER Together, shall us?
JOHN Oy. Together.

They look at each other, swallow, and, as on a beat, scramble up out of the hollow. Leaving four scared companions.

Scene 17

Trees beyond the hollow. Moving cautiously, and whispering, JOHN *and* PETER *move through the trees.*

JOHN (*Whispering*) If you hear anything—
PETER Yes? What?
JOHN We'll throw ourselves flat on the ground.
PETER What for?
JOHN That's what soldiers do.
PETER Yeh. Right.

Silently, they move forward in a comic parody of pantomimic creeping.

Scene 18

The hollow. The four left behind are tense and nervous.

WILLIE (*In a low voice*) I don't reckon they be safe out there. Him'll jump out on 'um.
ANGELA (*Close to tears again*) Will they come back?
AUDREY (*Snarling*) 'Course they will.

Silence. Birdsong.

WILLIE I don't trust 'em. I don't trust 'em at all. They'll run home for their dinner.
AUDREY Shhh!

They hold silence. Tense. Blackbird's warning trill. Suddenly a blood-curdling cry, off, through the trees.

JOHN (*Off*) No-o-o-oo-oo! Aaaaaaah! Him have got me! Aaaaagh! The knife!
PETER (*Off*) Keep away! Keep away! No-o-o-oo! Aaaaaa-aaaagh! I be done for!

Wide-eyed and trembling with shock and terror, WILLIE, RAYMOND, ANGELA *and* AUDREY *cling to each other, moaning and sobbing.*

Scene 19

Trees beyond the hollow. Out in the wood, PETER *and* JOHN *(who have decided that nobody is about) are rolling on the ground, helpless with suppressed, belly-aching laughter. A moment before either of them is able to speak.*

PETER (*Eventually*) Ho-hoo-hoo – do you – hee-hee.
JOHN Do I – ho-ho – do I – hee-hee-hee – do I what? Ho-ho-ho ...

They have to break off for more near hysterical laughter.

PETER (*At last*) Do you think – (*He gasps*) – do you think they heard?

JOHN They – they heard all right.

And both explode with helpless but suppressed laughter again.

Scene 20

The hollow. The four are in painful desperation. ANGELA *is weeping.* RAYMOND *has his hands to his ears, eyes screwed shut, moaning.* AUDREY *is curled up in foetal position and then* WILLIE:

WILLIE Help! Help! He-e-elp! Dad! Dad! Help!

The others decide to do the same.

ALL Help! Help! Help!

Scene 21

The old barn. 'DONALD DUCK' sits on the trough or cartwheel, striking matches one after another from a box of 'England's Glory'. He lets each match burn down until it almost reaches his fingers, then drops it quickly. All the time he glances round, anxiously. He strikes another match, watches the flame. A new expression flares in his eyes. He looks round at the heap of hay – so intently that the match burns his fingers.

DONALD Oh! (*He drops the match quickly*)

Scene 22

The hollow. The cries at peak desperation.

WILLIE
RAYMOND
AUDREY
ANGELA
} (*Together*) Help – help – help!

And the pram comes crashing down on top of them. Shrieking and shouting in panic, the four scramble up out of the hollow as fast as they can. To be met by PETER *and* JOHN, *pointing and whooping with delight and derision.*

JOHN Hee! Hee! Gotcha! Gotcha!
PETER Hoo! Hoo! Had ya – didn't us! Didn't us!

AUDREY goes wild. She leaps at PETER, *nails clawing, hands flailing.*

AUDREY You devil! You devil!

The violence of her momentum knocks PETER *to the ground.*

PETER Get off! Get – off!

But she pummels him hard. The others watch, open-mouthed.

AUDREY I'll bash you up! Bash you up! Bash you up!
PETER Ow! Ow! Ow! Audrey – no! No!
JOHN Girls ent s'posed to do that.
AUDREY Bash-you-up!
PETER Get off – off!

With a desperate heave, he rolls over on top of her and pinions her wrists.

JOHN Good old Peter!
PETER Give in? Going to stop?
AUDREY (*Shrill*) I shall tell our mam!

ANGELA Yes! And I ool!
JOHN Oh, come on. 'S only a bit of fun.
WILLIE Fun!
RAYMOND Wasn't very n-nun-nice for us!
PETER (*Gasping*) Give in? Audrey? Or I'll spit, mind! (*He makes a bubble of spit*)
AUDREY No!
PETER I'll spit on thee glasses, Aud. I will.
AUDREY (*Gasping*) I be a *girl*, mind. A girl!
ANGELA You dirty devil, Peter!
WILLIE (*Suddenly shouting and pointing*) Look! Look!

They all stop, and look.

JOHN What is it?
WILLIE (*Gurgling*) The Itie! And him have got a gurt long knife!

Frozen horror.

PETER (*Quaking*) W-where ...?

WILLIE *gives a gleeful little jig.*

WILLIE Gotcha! Gotcha!
PETER (*Furiously*) I shall smack thou one!
AUDREY See! See! 'Tent very nice, is it, biggie boots!
JOHN (*Just to be sure*) You didn't see nothing, did you?
WILLIE No. But I might have. Him might be there for all we do know.

The thought is extremely sobering for all of them.

RAYMOND P'raps him's l-lul-looking at us n-nun-now.
AUDREY Oh my God.
JOHN (*Frowning*) We have made a hell of a racket, ant us?
PETER Him might have heard.
WILLIE (*Twitching*) *Would* have heard.
ANGELA Oh let's get on home. Let's get away from here!

PETER Oy. We'd better. Shall us, John?
WILLIE Hadn't us, John?
JOHN (*Whispering*) Don't talk so loud.

They all look at each other.

PETER Come on! I byunt stopping. Let's run for it!

And without more ado he bolts. The six, in ragged formation, crash through ferns and undergrowth.

Scene 23

The old barn. DONALD DUCK *stooping down, a small pile of burnt-out matches beside him, strikes yet another, cups his hand to shield the flame, and tries to light the hay. It seems this is not the first attempt: some of the dampish hay is charred. And the flame flickers, flares, dies.*

DONALD (*Intense*) Aw, come on. Come on. (*He strikes another 'England's Glory'*) If it don't take this time, the Japs have won. The bloody flaming buggering flaming bloody buggering Japs have won! (*He holds it to the hay. A small flame flutters, almost dies, then very slowly curls and licks along the edge of the hay. Crackle-crackle-crackle. Excited now, jigging a bit, sucking on his fingers, he watches it. Then, with cupped hands, he feeds the little fire with some of the drier hay. Trance-like*) Come on, come on, come, come on, come.

And it is coming on.

Scene 24

Open ground, and field. JOHN, PETER, WILLIE, RAYMOND, ANGELA *and* AUDREY *out of breath, have run from the woods, across the common, into the field. The barn is up ahead. John slows.*

JOHN Oof! I be puffed!
PETER (*Gasping*) I could keep going for another hundred miles.
WILLIE (*Panting*) Oy, I'll bet.
ANGELA (*Gasping*) We kept up, didn't us?
AUDREY (*Panting*) My glasses is all steamed over.
RAYMOND (*Gasping*) F-Fuf-Four eyes.
AUDREY (*Singing*)

When the mum-moon shines
Over the cuc-cow shed—

JOHN Oh, stop arguing for God's sake. We be safe now, ben us? Too fast for thik bloody Itie any road!
PETER Wonder if Donald Duck is still hiding in the barn?
WILLIE Poor old Quack Quack.

They laugh.

RAYMOND Let's p-pup-pretend t-to ...
JOHN Be the I-talian. Oy. That's a good 'un!
PETER It have come off twice!
JOHN Three times lucky!
PETER (*Chortling*) Frighten him to death.
WILLIE (*Putting on a deep voice, mimics*) Who is-a da there! I gotta da knife-a!

They laugh in delight.

PETER (*Impressed*) That's good that is, Willie.
WILLIE (*Pleased*) You know, like Musso the Wop in the comic.
JOHN Creep up on him – eh? That's a good 'un.

PETER   Last one to the barn is a cissy!

And away he scampers.

Scene 25

The old barn. DONALD, *eyes smarting, stands back in awe at the size of the fire he has created. The flames are engulfing the greater mass of hay in about a quarter of the barn, and a few tongues of fire are stretching towards the roof. Eyes wide, mouth open,* DONALD *begins to back towards the door, which is kept half open by a large stone.*

DONALD   (*With hate*) Burn you bugger! Burn! Burn!

The flames seem to swell and belly out suddenly. DONALD, *in alarm, scurries for the door. And it slams shut – bang!*

Scene 26

Outside the barn. Giggling with excitement, the other six have slammed shut the door, putting the stone back against it, and further holding it shut with six pairs of hands.

WILLIE   (*Shouting*) Who – is – a – there! I gott-a da knife-a to slit-a da throat-a!

From inside, DONALD *is pushing against the door until it rattles.*

DONALD   (*Screaming, from inside*) Open the door! Help! Help!
PETER   (*Delighted*) Hark at him!

Rattle – thump – scream.

WILLIE   (*Shouting*) I gott-a da knife-a.
DONALD   (*Screaming, from inside*) Help! Help!

Smoke is seeping under the door.

JOHN   Him have got a fire going, the devil.
PETER   And him told me him didn't have no matches! Hark at him, though. Good, ennit?

They are all laughing.

DONALD   (*Screaming inside*) Open the door! Please! Please! Open the door! Plea-ea-ease!

Scene 27

The old barn. In a dreadful panic, and unable to think, DONALD *retreats from the door to try to get out of the window, trapping himself. The flames drive in a leaping crackle towards the door. As* DONALD, *wildly dashing about, screams, a roof timber collapses beside him in a shower of sparks.*

Scene 28

Outside the barn. Looks of consternation on six faces. WILLIE *is the first to realise fully.*

WILLIE   Quick! Quick!
JOHN   What? Wha –?
WILLIE   (*Sobbing*) Open the door! Open it!
ANGELA   (*Screaming*) Open it!

In a flustered frenzy they drag open the barn door. Flames leap out towards the air. They recoil in terror and horror, screaming and shouting.

WILLIE   (*Sobbing*) Donald! Donald! Oh Donald!
PETER   (*Crying*) Come on out! Donald! Come on, old pal!
JOHN   I shall tell his mam! I shall! Silly great fool!
WILLIE   Oh don't do that! No!
JOHN   (*Yelling*) I shall! I shall tell his mam!

ALL   Donald! Donald ...!

> DONALD *is briefly glimpsed through the flames, gesticulating, then wholly engulfed. The barn is being gutted, and the tiles slide off the roof. In terror, the six run away as the inside of the barn implodes into flame. They run, run, back into the tall grass of the field.*

Scene 29

The field. They sit, obscured by long grass, curiously apart, badly shaken.

RAYMOND   P-poor old Donald!
ANGELA   He should've – he should've come out ...!
AUDREY   'Twasn't our fault!
JOHN   We'll be sure to get the blame though. You can bank on it.
PETER   I byunt going to get the blame for it. I never did anything. I wasn't even holding the door.
ANGELA   Yes you were!
PETER   No I wasn't! I was bloody miles away!
AUDREY   You was with *me*, Peter. Wasn't you with me?

Pause

WILLIE   We was all together.
ANGELA   Miles away!

Pause

WILLIE   What?
ANGELA   Well, we were! Hiding in the trees, weren't we?
JOHN   That's right. We didn't see nothing.
PETER   (*Eagerly*) We don't know nothing about it, do us?

But they start to cry, overwhelmed.

RAYMOND   Poor old Quack Quack.

They sob while the barn burns.

VOICE Into my heart, an air that kills
From yon far country blows
What are those blue remembered hills?
What spires, what farms are those?
That is the land of lost content,
I see it shining plain.
The happy highways where I went
And cannot come again.

Put the Old Man Away

from the television episode *Homes Fit for Heroes*
in the series *Steptoe and Son* (1963)

by Ray Galton and Alan Simpson

Harold, in his thirties, and his elderly widowed father, Albert, depend on each other. They make a living in the streets of London in the early 1960s as 'totters' – buying and selling scrap materials and unwanted bits and pieces from people's homes. Harold has vague dreams of a more exciting life. Now he has a scheme to sail round the world. Albert fought in the 1914–18 war, in which one of the slogans, as peace appeared in sight, was the phrase used as the title of this episode: *Homes Fit for Heroes* – the idea of building a better world after the war. The 'home' in this episode is one into which Harold thinks he'll put his father while he takes to the seas. At the start of this extract, the television screen cuts from a grimy street in the town to the country.

Characters

HAROLD
ALBERT
OLD LADY, Miss Lotterby
MATRON

Out in the country

Long shot of the horse and cart, with HAROLD *driving and* ALBERT *next to him, going down a country lane.* HAROLD *is happily enjoying the country air.* ALBERT *is cold and miser-*

able. HAROLD *is talking in a rather put-on, phoney sort of way.*

HAROLD Oh, it is beautiful round here, isn't it?

ALBERT Let's go home, Harold. I'm frozen! What do you want to drag me all the way out here for?

HAROLD I thought you'd enjoy a nice drive out in the country on a Sunday afternoon. Do you good. You don't get out enough. Look at that view!

ALBERT Dah!

HAROLD Wouldn't you like to live round here?

ALBERT No, I wouldn't. I want to go home and get round the fire. There's good film on telly this afternoon.

HAROLD Wouldn't you really like to live round here? I mean, given the chance wouldn't you like to end your days in a place like this? Wouldn't you like to get away from that dirty old house and spend the rest of your life in these idyllic surroundings? You deserve it, Dad, after the hard life you've had. (ALBERT *looks at* HAROLD *suspiciously.* HAROLD *suddenly spots something*) Oh, just look at that house! (*Shot of a large country house*) Isn't that magnificent? Oh, pater, look at that! (*We look at* ALBERT) Who lives there? It must be a millionaire at least. Oh, what wouldn't you give to live in a place like that? Oh well, it's just fantastic, isn't it? Who could it belong to? Oh look, there's a notice board. I wonder what it says. (*Shot of a notice board, reading 'Chartwell House: Old People's Home'*) 'Chartwell House. Old People's Home.' Well, well, well. (*We look at* ALBERT) Who would have believed it? A beautiful place like that for an old people's home!

ALBERT I ain't going in!

HAROLD Now, Dad!

ALBERT Take me home! I ain't going in!

HAROLD Who said anything about ...?

ALBERT I wondered why you brought me out here. (*Mimics* HAROLD) 'Look at the lovely countryside! Oooh! What a lovely house! I wonder who that belongs to.' You conniving young ...! Take me home.

HAROLD But, Dad, listen....

ALBERT Take me home! Give us them reins! (ALBERT *grabs the reins*) Giddap!

The horse and cart go down the lane at a fast trot.

The Steptoes' living-room

Dissolve to ALBERT *stalking in, followed by* HAROLD. *A bright fire burns in the grate.*

HAROLD Dad, I assure you. It was sheer coincidence....

ALBERT I might have known you were up to something this morning, bringing me breakfast up on a tray. Slimy, that's what you are, conniving, and crafty. Just like your mother, God rest her soul.

HAROLD Dad, I had no idea....

ALBERT You haven't got the guts to say it to my face, have you? (*Standing by the table*) Can you look me straight in the eye and deny that you're trying to get me put in an old people's home?

We see first HAROLD, *then* ALBERT, *in close-up.* HAROLD *looks him straight in the eye.* ALBERT *looks steadily back as they stare at each other. After a few seconds* HAROLD's *gaze weakens and he averts his eyes. The camera zooms in on* ALBERT, *realising that it's true and he sinks into his chair by the table.* HAROLD *is embarrassed. He goes over to his cocktail cabinet and pours himself a drink.*

HAROLD Would you like a drink? (ALBERT *doesn't reply. He just stares at* HAROLD) Don't look at me like that! Look, it's not my fault. It's like what they said in the *Guardian* the other week. You are a victim of the failure of Western society in not knowing how to take care of their old people.

ALBERT (*Aggressively*) I'm not old. I could still have you over.

HAROLD *continues getting a drink.*

HAROLD All right then. Let's say their senior citizens. You see, they don't have this problem in the East. The family unit is still very strong out there. They've managed to solve the problem. It's all tied up with Shinto.[1] They worship their ancestors. (HAROLD*'s manner changes from being intellectual as we look at* ALBERT *again*) But we ain't wogs, Dad, we're English.

ALBERT Oh, it's religion now is it? All right then. What about honour thy father and thy mother?

HAROLD (*Finishing getting his drink, and moving slowly to the table*) Believe me, Dad, I'm only thinking of you. I haven't come to this decision lightly. If there was any other way out, I'd take it. But I'm afraid there is no other solution. I'm very sorry, but there it is. You've got to go.

ALBERT Why?

HAROLD (*Sitting down at the table*) Because I shall be going away very shortly, and you'll be left here on your own.

ALBERT (*Looking very alarmed*) Going away?

HAROLD Yeah.

ALBERT Where are you going?

HAROLD I'm going round the world on a sloop.

ALBERT You're doing what?

HAROLD I'm going round the world on a sloop. (ALBERT *starts laughing.* HAROLD *is angry*) What are you laughing at?

ALBERT (*Laughing heartily*) Oh gawd! Oh dear, oh dear!

HAROLD (*Sounding very aggrieved*) I don't see what's funny

---

[1] an old Japanese religion

about that. Lots of people do it. It's adventure. It's, it's doing something.

ALBERT (*Weak with laughter*) Oh stop it! No stop it, Harold! Oooh my heart! Oh dear!

HAROLD (*Very incensed*) Stop it! Stop laughing! (ALBERT *gradually subsides. Occasionally he chuckles. He almost starts to go off again, but stops himself. He wipes his eyes.* HAROLD *is very much on his dignity*) If you think by ridiculing me you're going to make me change my mind, you've got another thing coming. There is nothing you can do about it. I am going round the world on a sloop and that is all there is to it.

ALBERT So that's what you bought a new suit for?

HAROLD Yeah.

ALBERT (*No longer laughing*) You're not serious?

HAROLD I am dead serious, mate.

ALBERT In that case, it's you should be going in a home, not me. You great big berk! You want your brains tested!

HAROLD I know what's wrong with you! You're jealous, aren't you? Just because you ain't been nowhere you don't want me to go.

ALBERT I've travelled, mate.

HAROLD Travelled? Bognor every year? Peering out of the bay window of a boarding house for fourteen days?

ALBERT I been abroad. France.

HAROLD Oh yes, I forgot about that. Four years in a trench and a fortnight in Bognor. A world authority on travel. A proper little Marco Polo,[2] ain't you?

ALBERT I've travelled enough to know it's all the same.

HAROLD How can it be the same? How can India be the same as this? I want to see it mate. Before I die, I want to

---

[2] one of the first Europeans to write about his travels in Central Asia and China

ALBERT	see the dawn come up like thunder. I don't want to read about it, I want to hear it. I want to sit round the camp fire with a bunch of Sheikhs sorting through the rice for a couple of sheep's eyes.
ALBERT	Ugh!

As HAROLD *goes on he moves to a large geographer's globe of the world. He sits at the desk next to the globe.*

HAROLD The Taj Mahal, the Barrier Reef, the Hanging Gardens of Babylon, the Seven Pillars of Wisdom, the Grapes of Wrath. It's just the same ain't it? Yeah, you can see all that down the Bingo Hall, can't you?

ALBERT Dah!

HAROLD I don't want to get as old as you and look back and think, what have I done? Nothing! Where have I been? Nowhere! I want to be able to look back and say 'Oh yeah, nineteen-seventy-one, that was when I was a gaucho on the Pampas, rounding up steers.' I want to see their eyes light up when I tell them about going round the Horn with everything lashed down, calling in at some tropical island for fresh water, garlands hung round my neck, by dusky, slant-eyed maidens, stretched out on some palm-fringed beach eating bread fruit, pearl fishing in the Coral Sea, ivory smuggling up the coast of Africa, whale hunting off Antarctica. (*He is now gazing into the distance, quite carried away*)

ALBERT (*With a sneer on his face*) Shipwrecked off Southend that's about as far as you'll get.

HAROLD (*In a harsh, superior voice*) Can we say that will be the last of your senile attempts at humour for today?

ALBERT Well, pull yourself together. What do you know about boats? How could you sail round the world in a sloop on your own?

HAROLD (*Still superior*) I am not going on my own. Obviously I wouldn't attempt a voyage like that on my own. I am not stupid. There's ten of us. Five blokes and five birds.

ALBERT *nods very knowingly.*

ALBERT Oh, now we're getting down to it. It's one of those dos, is it?

HAROLD It is not 'one of those dos'. What a vulgar, dirty little mind you've got! This is a perfectly serious attempt by a bunch of *young* people to explore the world around us. (ALBERT *looks very unconvinced*) If you must know, I have answered a perfectly respectable advert in the *New Statesman*. He's got his own boat and he wants nine other people in search of adventure to join him on an expedition round the world. I realise it's a bit hard for people of your generation to understand, but, believe me, it's not unusual in these days. They're all doing it. It's the Outward Bound school, Dad. They're not content just sitting round the television set watching 'Bonanza'. They want to be in it. They're off. They're climbing mountains because they're there. They're doing things.

ALBERT What does he want five birds for?

HAROLD Oh Dad, don't be so suburbanly preoccupied with sex, for gawd's sake! These are highly intelligent people. They don't look at it like that. It's just five people going on a trip with five other people.

ALBERT Why don't you have ten blokes then?

HAROLD Well I don't know. I'm not organising the trip. Perhaps he thought that....

ALBERT (*Knowingly*) Yeah, I know what he thought.

HAROLD (*Resignedly*) Oh, there's no point in talking to you. If you like to think of it as a sex orgy on the high seas, that's up to you. It's just another example of the gulf between our two generations, that's all. A thing like this would have been impossible in your day.

ALBERT (*Imagining it*) That's true. Five men and five women on a boat! There wouldn't have been much sailing done, I can tell you.

HAROLD Sometimes you disgust me! Surely there are pursuits that men and women can do together without sex coming into it? All I can say is it will be a sad day for the world when a bird can't go mountain-climbing with a bloke without being got at on a precipice. Anyway, there's no point in discussing it further. It's all arranged. We'll be setting sail next month.

ALBERT (*Starting to sound pathetic*) I see. I'm going to be bunged into an old people's home while you float round the world with five bits of crumpet.

HAROLD (*Trying to sound firm but kind*) I don't intend to enter into a slanging match with you. I've been as fair as I can. I shall arrange to dispose of the business and you can have the entire proceeds. I don't want a penny of it.

ALBERT (*Still pathetic*) And a lot I'll have to spend it on, won't I? Sitting in that home for the rest of me life, playing dominoes and making handbags. Very nice! (ALBERT *slowly gets up from his chair*) I don't think I want to stay down here with you any more. I think I'll go up to me room.

ALBERT *moves over towards the door.* HAROLD *is hurt at this and gets up from the chair by the desk.*

HAROLD (*Pleading*) Dad, don't take it like this. You don't have to go up yet. I was just going to make some supper.

ALBERT *goes out into the hall and starts to climb the stairs.* HAROLD *stands in the doorway.*

ALBERT (*From the stairs*) Don't you do anything for me. I couldn't eat it. It'd stick in my throat. I don't want anything more from you.

HAROLD (*Rather desperately*) Don't think you're going to make me feel rotten about it! My conscience is clear. I've spent my life looking after you. I could have gone years ago. Most blokes would have.

ALBERT (*From the stairs*) There's one thing that cheers me up about all this.

HAROLD (*Hopefully*) What's that?

ALBERT (*From the stairs*) That the whole bleeding crowd of you might get drowned.

HAROLD moves back into the living-room from the door. He goes to the wardrobe and takes out a sextant. He returns to the desk, unrolls a map of the world and marks his voyage across it. He smiles with anticipation, looking into the brightly burning fire, as the scene fades out.

The drive of Chartwell House Old People's Home

We fade up on the horse and cart with the two Steptoes aboard going in the gates of the home. It stops outside the front door. HAROLD *and* ALBERT *get down.* HAROLD *takes down two suitcases.* ALBERT *is dressed in his best clothes. They go up the steps and into the mansion.*

Inside Chartwell House

Dissolve to the Reception Hall of the home. HAROLD *and* ALBERT *enter.* HAROLD *puts down the bags. They are old battered suitcases, tied up with a bit of string.* HAROLD *nods to* ALBERT*'s hat.* ALBERT *takes it off. His hair is smartly brushed. Some old people walk past.* ALBERT *watches them.*

HAROLD Did you notice the gardens? You used to like gardening, didn't you. Remember that window box you used to have? (*The old man doesn't want to know.* HAROLD *goes over to the notice board. He stands reading the notices*) Oooh! Listen to this. 'Entertainments programme:

Monday night, whist.
Tuesday night, a film matinee.
Wednesday night, whist.
Thursday, a recital of old English madrigals by the Egthorpe Amateur Choral Society.
Friday night, whist.
Saturday, a coach outing. A mystery tour round Berkshire.'

(ALBERT *looks very unimpressed*) I think we've been very lucky to get you in here. You're a very fortunate old man.

ALBERT I hope the sharks get you.
HAROLD (*Whispering urgently*) Father, behave yourself. Don't start a punch-up in here.
ALBERT (*Not whispering*) Why not? Let them know what sort of a son I've got. Go on! Clear off! I'm in, that's what you wanted. You get off down to your sloop.
HAROLD (*Trying to sound kind*) Not till I've seen you settled in. Don't make things difficult. Ssshhh! Somebody's coming!

HAROLD *beams as an old lady approaches the two men.*

OLD LADY Good morning. Were you looking for somebody?
HAROLD Oh yes ma'am. We're looking for the matron. This is my father. He's coming to stay here.
OLD LADY Good! New blood, that's what we need here. (*She smiles at* ALBERT) My name is Lotterby, Miss Lotterby. Games and extramural activities. Once you're settled in I'll pop along to your room and see what you're interested in. (ALBERT *turns and looks at* HAROLD, *surprised, then back at* MISS LOTTERBY) See you at lunch.

MISS LOTTERBY *goes off.*

HAROLD (*Whispering*) I do believe she fancies you. You're going to be all right there. I think you're going to have a ball here.

ALBERT *looks sourly at him. The* MATRON *comes up.*

MATRON (*Very brightly*) Ah, good morning, Mr Steptoe.
HAROLD Good morning, Matron.
MATRON So this is the old gentleman.
ALBERT (*Aggressively*) I'm not an old gentleman. And we might as well get it straight from the start, I'm in here against my will. I want it to go down in my folder, 'Here under protest!'
MATRON I'm sure your son is only doing what's best for you. I know you'll be very happy here.
ALBERT I won't!
MATRON Yes, you will!
ALBERT I won't! I'm a trouble-maker! I'm warning you. I'm always ringing bells in the middle of the night. He knows that. I've been in hospital. I'm fussy about me food, and if I don't get what I want I'm liable to go on hunger strike. (*Pause*) You get old ladies here, haven't you? (ALBERT *looks leeringly at the* MATRON)
MATRON Yes.
ALBERT Well you'd better keep them locked up for a start.
HAROLD (*Anxiously*) He's harmless really. He's quite a sweet old man when you get to know him.
ALBERT (*To* MATRON) He's going round the world with a boatload of birds. Dirty little beast!
HAROLD (*Still anxiously*) Don't you listen to him.
MATRON (*In a motherly voice to* HAROLD) Don't worry, Mr Steptoe. I understand. They're always a bit upset at first. We'll take care of him. He'll be in good hands. Come along, I'll show you to your room. This way.

The Steptoes follow her across the lounge, HAROLD *carrying the suitcases. There are several old people sitting around. They look up and smile as* HAROLD *and* ALBERT *go past.* HAROLD *smiles charmingly. The old man just glares at them.*

ALBERT (*Muttering*) Bags!

The Hundred Nights

from the Japanese Noh play
Sotoba Komachi (14th century)

(adapted from a variety of translations by Michael Marland)

Most modern plays mimic real life and try to look like a sequence of events that could really have happened. The Japanese Noh theatre looked down on such direct imitation. Instead, five or six related pieces celebrated the achievements and sadnesses of life. They are partly in verse and partly in prose. Often 'chorus' figures speak a commentary, and even describe the feelings of the main characters.

In this, a very old woman struggles through the night. She remembers her cruelty to her lover very many years ago. The performers take their place on a platform, with a chorus in a semicircle speaking to the audience. Single voices could take the speeches marked 'All Chorus', 'Chorus A' and 'Chorus B'; or a group could rehearse to recite these together, half the group reciting 'Chorus A' and half 'Chorus B'.

Characters

CHORUS
FIRST VOICE
SECOND VOICE
KOMACHI, a very old woman
THIRD VOICE
FOURTH VOICE
FIFTH VOICE

The CHORUS *stand in a semicircle.*

ALL CHORUS Evening:

Men's eyes peer to make out the turns in the path.
The thick, warm air lies heavy and still,
But the shadows grow and move with the moon.

1ST VOICE That creeping shadow there! Can it be a withered bough?

2ND VOICE No. It is the crumpled form of a woman, dragging herself along.

CHORUS A It is that old beggar woman
Who lives up in the quiet hills
Shunning the company of men,
Unknown and unvisited.

CHORUS B But today she's been down to the capital
To beg at the shrines and sanctuaries.
She must have woken when the dawn lay lemon on the hemp fields,
Left her mattress of straw and toiled down to the plain,
Passing the fields where men were working,
And the great ox sweating at the plough, under the now vertical sun,
Reaching the world of men and their money.

Enter KOMACHI, *an old bent woman dressed in rags, with a bundle, basket and pouch hanging from her neck.*

ALL CHORUS Now in the dark she hobbles out of the city
West with the eyeless moon.
No guard would challenge such a wretched traveller,
Yet still she slinks in the shadows, under the trees,
Furtive as a rat.
She goes past the Lovers' Tomb; past the Hill of Autumn;

And here now is the river, the river of Katsura,
Boats and the glare of moonlight.

KOMACHI, *at the front of the stage, peers out at the river.*

KOMACHI I listen for the whisper of the ebbing tide,
But hear nothing.
If I could find it I would let it carry me in its flow,
Like an old dead reed cut out from its root.
It was different once: I was more than this husk that I am;
I was young, I was proud.
My hair was as fresh as spring leaves;
Supple as the willow I walked with the wind in my hair,
The spring wind.
My voice was nightingales among the branches.
My body bloomed tender as a dog-rose.
Now when I go by even the sluts turn away;
I am old, a hundred years, and each day older.
I fear men's eyes in the city lest they recognise me:
'Is that her,' their friends would say, 'whose beauty we have heard of so often?'

She shrinks back from the moonlight, covering her face.

Who are they rowing in these boats?
Are they men, those black shadows, or death's fishermen?
Would they take me in their boats, towing out west on the ebb-tide?
Why don't they turn and come for me? Why won't they take me?
Why do they only row smaller and smaller into the darkness without me?
They have forgotten me.

But I am too tired to go further, and there's nowhere further to go.
So let me sit down on this old stump.

She sits wearily down to one side of the stage.

3RD VOICE Just look at that old beggar woman now! That tree she's sitting on is a sacred shrine!

4TH VOICE Old woman do you realise you're sitting on a sacred shrine? Show some decent respect and get yourself off!

KOMACHI (*Rising slowly*) A sacred shrine? There's nothing on it to say so, no letters, or painting, or carved figures that I can see. I thought it was an old tree-stump.

3RD VOICE Just an old tree-stump!

4TH VOICE It still has the sacred sign imprinted on it.

KOMACHI Well, I am only an old stump too.

5TH VOICE Who are you? Something in your voice makes me want to know your name. Who are you?

4TH VOICE If we know your name we will pray for you when you are dead. Who are you?

KOMACHI Pray for me then:
For I am the ruins of Ono,
The daughter of Ono Yoshizane.
I am Ono Komachi.
Write me in your prayer list.

ALL CHORUS Can this be Komachi? In her day she was a bright flower.

KOMACHI *puts her young mask before her face.*

1ST VOICE Her brows were like two young moons;
Her eyes as clear as the blue waters of the Katsura.

2ND VOICE She used no powder at all.
Each day in different robes she walked in palaces.

3RD VOICE Many listened to her verses;

SOTOBA KOMACHI

> Some were in her native tongue, and some in that of a foreign country.

4TH VOICE At feasts she drank from a brilliant cup;
And the gleam of it dropped like moonlight on her sleeve.

KOMACHI lowers her youthful mask.

> So has her splendour dropped from her
> White of winter covers her head;
> She has lost her black, coiled hair, softer than the night,
> And silted seaweed locks hang now on her wilted flesh.

KOMACHI Cover from the cold dawn my dull hairs;
Hide the shame that rests on my head.

KOMACHI lifts her cloak over her head.

1ST VOICE What is in that pouch hanging from your neck?
KOMACHI A few dried beans and a cake of millet.
For hunger will come if death does not.
2ND VOICE And that bundle on your back?
KOMACHI A few old rags to do for clothing.
3RD VOICE What is in the basket that you carry?
KOMACHI Prayer offerings.
ALL CHORUS She cannot hide her face from our eyes.
She cannot protect her limbs from the dew,
Nor from rain, nor frost, nor snow.

KOMACHI mimes the following actions.

> Not rags enough to wipe her old eyes with!
> She wanders along the roads, begging from anyone that passes.
> And when they give her nothing
> She is gripped by a kind of crazy rage,
> Her voice changes as if a spirit possessed her!

KOMACHI imagines some passers-by, puts her hands out to them and shrieks menacingly.

KOMACHI Give me something, you smug priests! Give me something! Give ...

She is possessed by the spirit of her lover, Shojho.

1ST VOICE What do you want?
KOMACHI (*Speaking as Shojho*) Komachi! Let me go to Komachi!
2ND VOICE But you told us you were Komachi! Are you out of your wits?

KOMACHI puts on the mask of Shojho.

KOMACHI Komachi? How should I be Komachi?
Komachi is beautiful.
She receives many messages of love;
Letters come thick and fast as raindrops in a summer storm.
But she sends no answers, not a word in return.
And now she is punished with age.
She is old.
A hundred years she has lived –
I loved her; I love Komachi.

3RD VOICE But you are Komachi. Whose spirit has possessed you?

KOMACHI There were many who loved her, many loved Komachi,
But of all of them it was Shojho who loved her best,
Shii no Shojho the Captain.

ALL CHORUS She said she would not hear him
Until he had travelled from his distant home,
Had travelled a hundred times on foot
And each time carved a new mark on the shaft-bench.

The tedious miles of the foot-track stretched before
   him,
But Shojho the Captain had eyes
For nothing but his travels' end.

Turn back the wheel of Shojho's sadness.
Let it be lived again.

KOMACHI *is robed in the travelling cloak of Shojho.*

He travels again to the shaft-bench
The slow sun times the day. What is the time?
Evening. Now he walks alone through the
   moonlight.
There are guards posted, but no guards will stop
   him!
Lifting up his heavy travelling cloak,
Pulling up his hood to cover him,
Hidden from men's eyes, he went to her.
Through the moonlight, and through the black,
Through the beating rain, through the wind full of
   torn leaves
Through the grey, wet snow,
When the water dripped, dripped from the eaves;
Swiftly going, swiftly returning.
Going, returning; One night, two nights, three
   nights,
(The tenth night, it is said, was harvest night.)
Going to her, yet never seeing her.

Like the daily clock marking the clockwork dawn,
Each day he carved the new mark on the
   shaft-bench
As she had commanded.
She said he must come a hundred times before she
   would hear him
And time and again he came, time and again;

> As often as the water drops from the eaves,
> Ninety-nine times he came ...

KOMACHI *struggles in the death agonies of Shojho.*

KOMACHI   Is it snow blinding my eyes?
　　　　 Am I torn leaves to feel such pain?

KOMACHI *struggles and dies.*

ALL CHORUS   Such pain!
　　　　　　Before that hundredth night had passed,
　　　　　　He died – Shii no Shojho the Captain.
　　　　　　And now her punishment of age has ended:
　　　　　　His spirit has clutched her,
　　　　　　His anger has crazed her wits;
　　　　　　She has died as he had died
　　　　　　And her hundredth year has ended.

Farewell to the Memories of Life

from the stage play *Johnson over Jordan* (1939)

by J. B. Priestley

One of Britain's major playwrights of the twentieth century and also a very successful novelist and essayist, J. B. Priestley successfully wrote realistic plays that were very popular, such as *Dangerous Corner*, *Eden End* and *An Inspector Calls*. His sense of realism and his sense of humour led to plays that convinced audiences that 'this could really have happened'. However, he had in him also that sense of theatre as fantasy and that other strand of the century's drama: putting real characters in unreal situations. He saw the play on the stage as an important artistic contribution to the regeneration of the world.

In some Tibetan beliefs there is a time after death in which a dead person does not know that she or he no longer has a body of flesh and blood – a time when the recently dead person mistakes thoughts for actual realities. This stage between life and death was called 'Bardo'. Priestley's idea in *Johnson over Jordan* is to give 'an account, in dramatic form, of a man's life in a new way, taking an ordinary middle-class citizen of our time ... and giving to my record of his rather commonplace ordinary life an unusual depth and poignancy'. Priestley saw the use of this Bardo stage as showing the chief character 'discovering his best self and those things which had quickened his mind and touched his heart'. The play uses dance and music, and many of the actors wear masks. He declared that by 'using heightened speech' he would 'break away from the flavourless patter of modern realistic dialogue'.

As we join the play, Johnson has passed through the first stages following his death, and he has been purged by terror and remorse. He reaches an inn where he will say goodbye to everything familiar and of this life, before going out to a new adventure of living. Two days after the funeral, his daughter says to her mother that she seems to have shaken off her grief. Johnson's widow replies: 'You see, I know. I suddenly saw – quite clearly – everything's all right – really all right – now.'

Characters

ROBERT JOHNSON
PORTER, at the inn
WOMAN'S VOICE
ALBERT GOOP, a waiter
TOM, a teenage boy, Johnson's brother
MR MORRISON, a schoolmaster
DON QUIXOTE, the character from Cervantes' book
Various voices

As Johnson's widow smiles at her children, the light fades quickly, the scene goes, as we hear the music again, first rather sombre but then quickening to a delicious little tune ... We still hear the tune softly as we look at the Inn, which seems – as we shall soon hear it is – a rum place. At one side a long staircase comes down, almost at right angles to our line of sight, and underneath this staircase, where it makes a little wall, facing us, is a kind of cosy corner, with a small dining-table and some chairs, some bookshelves let into the wall, a curtained window, and a few framed photographs and small oldish pictures. On the other side is a large window, through which light is streaming. Farther back there does not seem to be anything very much – we merely have a vague impression of a high curtain making a shadowy back wall. JOHNSON *enters, wearing a thick travelling overcoat and underneath that a country suit. He is just removing his bowler hat. Behind him there enters the inn* PORTER, *a stalwart, pleasant-faced fellow, who is carrying* JOHNSON's *small bag.* JOHNSON *looks about him, still bewildered but now quite pleasantly bewildered.*

PORTER Now, sir, I'll put your bag and coat where I can lay hands on 'em the minute they're wanted.

JOHNSON (*Handing over his hat and coat*) Good!

PORTER (*Who has taken the coat*) Nice thick coat too, sir – and you're quite right, for it gets cold here late at night. High up, you see, that's what we are – high up, Mr Johnson.

JOHNSON (*Surprised*) How do you know my name?

PORTER (*Smiling*) Oh – we were expecting you.

JOHNSON But I don't see how you could have been expecting me.

PORTER (*Who is perhaps more artful than he looks*) Why, sir, don't you like being expected?

JOHNSON Well – yes – I suppose we all do.

PORTER (*As if that settles it*) Well, there you are, sir.

JOHNSON *gives him a puzzled glance, then moves down a pace or two, looking about him. Then he sees the* PORTER *is still waiting, as if for a tip, and so feels in his pockets.*

JOHNSON Oh – er – sorry. I don't seem to have any money with me.

PORTER (*Coming forward again*) That's all right, sir. Don't take money here. No use for it. But – there's other and better ways of saying 'Thank you', y'know, sir.

JOHNSON (*Staring at him*) I don't understand you. (*Then, with sudden recognition*) Here, but wait a minute! I know you.

PORTER (*Pleased*) Ah – now then, you're talking, sir. And that's what we like here. No money – but just what you did now, sir – letting your face light up.

JOHNSON (*Triumphantly*) I know – I know!

PORTER (*Chuckling*) Are you sure, sir?

JOHNSON (*Triumphantly*) Yes, of course I am. You're Jim Kirkland.

PORTER Right, sir. Dead right!

JOHNSON (*All happy reminiscence*) Why, Jim, you were one of my great heroes. Good Lord! – I remember my father taking me to the Lancashire match for my birthday treat – I must have been about twelve – and I saw you make a hundred and seventy-eight not out. What an innings! Comes back to me now, clear as crystal. A smoking hot morning in July. I can smell the tar on the streets. I can taste the ginger-beer I had. I can still see your bat flashing in the sun. What a day! Jim Kirkland – (*He shakes hands with boyish enthusiasm*) This is a great moment for me.

PORTER Proud and happy, sir, proud and happy!

JOHNSON There's a poem about old cricketers, Jim. Did you ever read it? How did it end? 'As the run-stealers flicker to and fro, to and fro – Oh – my Hornby and my Barlow long ago.'

PORTER That's it, sir. Well – (*As if about to go*)

JOHNSON But what are you doing here?

PORTER (*Smiling*) Why, sir, meeting you. (*Confidentially*) It's a rum place, this, you'll see.

JOHNSON (*Dropping his voice a little*) I know. That window. Already, outside, it keeps changing.

He looks towards the corner under the staircase, and as soon as he does this a warm light illuminates this corner and the little pictures and photographs seem to glow.

JOHNSON And I'm sure some of these pictures and photographs – (*Goes to examine them*) Why, that's the photograph we had taken at school. I haven't seen it for over thirty years. (*Sees others*) And this used to be in my bedroom at home. It's the very same one. And that. No – this wasn't at home – it was at my grandfather's – I used to stare at it for hours – Good Lord! – I know them all, every one. That one I bought myself, first I ever bought – cost me twelve-and-six at a little second-hand shop. You're right, Jim – (*He turns round*) This *is* a –

But the PORTER *has gone.* JOHNSON *is bewildered. We hear, very faintly, the children's prayer theme from Humperdinck's opera.* JOHNSON *sits down, and now a woman's voice is heard, as if reading to a child.*

WOMAN'S VOICE Near a great forest there lived a poor woodcutter with his wife and his two children. The boy was called Hansel and the girl Gretel. The woodcutter was very poor indeed, and once when there was a famine in that land he could no longer give his wife and children their daily bread ...

JOHNSON (*Sharply, unconsciously*) Mother!

But the voice has stopped. A little waiter has appeared, an oldish chap with white hair and a droll, withered-apple face, and as soon as we have a good look at him we can see the old-clown look he has. He has one of those rusty Cockney voices so many of the old comedians had, and his name is ALBERT GOOP.

ALBERT Mr Johnson, isn't it, sir?
JOHNSON Yes.
ALBERT (*Smiling*) You'll find everything ready, sir, when you are. The lady was in early, telling me what you liked.
JOHNSON (*Surprised*) The lady?

ALBERT Yes, sir, *your* lady. (*Now, with deliberate comical air*) So you'll find everything in good trim. I say you'll find everything in good trim.

JOHNSON (*Staring at him*) I say – now – wait a minute—

ALBERT (*Who can't wait*) Yes, sir. Albert Goop. In pantomimes at the old Theatre Royal.

JOHNSON (*Triumphantly*) Of course!

ALBERT (*Almost doing his old act now*) Right, sir. And don't forget the little cane. (*Produces one*) I say don't forget the little cane.

JOHNSON You used to be the Baron in *Cinderella* and the Captain of the ship in *Robinson Crusoe*, and you always had your little cane, and said things twice. I used to spend hours and hours imitating you when I was a kid. Why, we all worshipped you, Albert Goop!

ALBERT (*Completely the comedian now, doing steps and everything*) Every Christmas at the old Theatre Royal, Longfield, there was Albert with his cane and a big red nose. Ah – happy days, sir, happy days!

JOHNSON Lord! – I'd count the weeks to those pantomimes – and the next sight of you, Albert.

ALBERT (*Doing a droll step*) Thank you very much. (*And now* JOHNSON *says it with him and does the step too*) I say thank you very much.

JOHNSON *laughs, then stares in astonishment out of the window, finally grinning like a schoolboy.*

JOHNSON Albert – I distinctly saw a stage-coach go down that road – and I'll swear Mr Pickwick was on it, with Sam Weller – and – I think – fat old Mr Weller was driving. What do you think about that, Albert?

ALBERT Doesn't surprise me. I say it doesn't surprise me. You can see anything through that window. I once saw 'alf the bill at the old Middlesex through it – Dan Leno, R. G. Knowles, Lottie Collins, everybody – then –

gone like a puff o' smoke – I say gone like a puff o' smoke.

JOHNSON By Jove, Albert – you know, Jim Kirkland's right. It's a rummy place this.

ALBERT Rum! It's the rummest you ever saw, this is. Why, it hasn't started on you yet. You wait – I say you wait.

JOHNSON Wait for what, Albert?

ALBERT Now don't ask questions, sir. Just let things happen. That's the way to go on here, sir – just let things happen.

JOHNSON Then I'll wait for the lady, Albert.

ALBERT She'll appreciate it, sir. I say she'll appreciate it.

They are now standing together near the foot of the stairs, and from farther up the stairs we hear the sound of a boy's voice. They both look up.

BOY'S VOICE Well, where is he then? I want to talk to him.

JOHNSON (*Startled*) Why, that's Tom's voice.

ALBERT Your brother, sir.

JOHNSON Yes, but he was killed in the War—

ALBERT (*Baffled*) War? What war?

TOM *comes running down the stairs. He is a fine-looking lad in his middle teens, dressed in the style of thirty-five years ago.*

TOM Bob, you chump! Now then, Albert, buzz off – this is private. (ALBERT *goes*) Just like you, Bob, to be so slow. You ought to have known this is the place to be in. Always keep me waiting, you old fathead.

JOHNSON (*Slowly, rather painfully*) Sorry, Tom. I didn't – well, I suppose I didn't know the way—

TOM (*Indicating the window*) Look there!

JOHNSON (*Staring*) Why – it's exactly what we used to see from our bedroom at that farm we stayed at those three summers. Look – the two haystacks – the road

                    dipping down – the pond we had the raft on – that
                    old cart—
TOM   The one you fell off, you ass.
JOHNSON   (*A boy again*) Well, don't forget you fell in the pond.

As he looks again, we hear the music JOHNSON *listened to in the office, and now the girl's voice comes in again, high and trailing.* JOHNSON *listens – then speaks very quietly.*

JOHNSON   I've heard that before, in the strangest places, and it
                    never lasts long. But at least it seems to belong here,
                    and it never did anywhere before.
TOM   What are you talking about?
JOHNSON   Didn't you hear it?
TOM   I didn't hear anything. Oh – Lord! – look who's here.

MORRISON, *a pleasant-looking, middle-aged schoolmaster, wearing an old blazer and smoking a pipe, has just entered, in the corner by the staircase, and now the warm light comes on there.*

JOHNSON   (*Turning*) Mr Morrison!
MORRISON   (*Coolly*) Hello! Both Johnsons at once.
TOM   Yes, sir, but I'm pushing off. See you later, Bob.
JOHNSON   (*With sudden urgency*) Tom!
TOM   (*Cheerfully, in a hurry, going upstairs*) All right, chump,
                    I'll see you later. I want to talk to old funny-face
                    upstairs about some bait he promised me.
JOHNSON   (*Going to foot of stairs and calling, distressed*) Tom! Tom!
MORRISON   (*As* JOHNSON *slowly comes nearer*) Tom's had enough of
                    my company. I'm afraid he doesn't like school-
                    masters, even out of hours. (*Pausing, then noting*
                    JOHNSON'*s distress*) Hello, what's worrying you,
                    Robert?
JOHNSON   (*With an effort*) It was – only seeing Tom again – after
                    so long a time—
MORRISON   Ah – there's none of that time here, y'know. You

must have brought a bit of it with you. Odd place this, Robert. Noticed the books?

JOHNSON (*In boyish tones*) No, sir.

MORRISON (*Smiling*) And I imagined I'd taught you to appreciate good literature. Have a look.

JOHNSON (*Going up to the books*) Why, they're all my old ones. Here's my old copy of *Don Quixote*. (*Turns the pages*) With all the pictures. I remember the first time I read this. It was one Christmas, a real snowy Christmas, and I'd had to go to bed with a snivelling cold – and I remember curling up in bed, very cosy, with the snow thickening on the window panes and the cold blue daylight dying – and first starting at the pictures ...

As he stands there, saying this, with the book in his hand, the light in that corner fades rapidly, and a bright moonlight streams through the window opposite, and we hear a lance tapping at the sill. The next moment DON QUIXOTE, *wearing old armour but no headpiece, is standing there, his white hair and beard and long, lined, fantastic face very sharply defined by the light, which also catches* JOHNSON's *face in a moment or two, when he steps forward.*

DON QUIXOTE (*Gravely*) Your pardon, sirs, but this night should bring to me one of the most famous adventures that ever was seen, for this whole region abounds with wicked enchanters and there are great wrongs to be redressed ...

JOHNSON (*Stepping forward eagerly*) Yes, just the same. Don Quixote, you don't know me, but I remember you.

DON QUIXOTE I seem to remember a boy in an upstairs room of a small house, far away, one winter's night—

JOHNSON (*Eagerly*) Yes, I was that boy. But I didn't think you'd remember.

DON QUIXOTE (*With a noble breadth*) Sir, your imagination, your memory of us, your affection for us, these are our life – all that we have.

JOHNSON Yes, I think I understand that.

DON QUIXOTE Your great poet once said that the best of our kind are but shadows, though I think he knew that your kind too – who appear so solid to yourselves for a little time – are also only shadows. And perhaps you too take life from the mind that beholds you and your little tale, so that you live as we must do, in another and greater being's imagination, memory and affection. (*Pauses*) Do you notice any change in me?

JOHNSON (*Gently hesitatingly*) Only – perhaps – you seem a trifle older—

DON QUIXOTE (*Sadly*) Yes. You see, we are being forgotten. We are shadows even to shadows, and play in a dream within a dream.

JOHNSON (*With feeling*) I am glad to have seen you, Don Quixote.

DON QUIXOTE (*In new and ringing tone*) Sir, I take life from your remembrance. If you should see my squire, Sancho Panza, tell him to follow me instantly along the highroad. Farewell, good sirs.

He salutes them and disappears. The bright moonlight goes with him, and now JOHNSON *is back in the lighted corner, looking at the books again.*

JOHNSON Yes, yes. They're all my old ones. *Grimm's Fairy Tales*. The *Arabian Nights* I used to crayon. The Shakespeare I had at school with you.

As he stands there, with MORRISON, *looking at the books, we hear voices, masculine and feminine, not coming from any one place, speaking famous lines.*

A VOICE	Daffodils, That come before the swallow dares and take The winds of March with beauty ...
ANOTHER VOICE	Will no one tell me what she sings? Perhaps the plaintive numbers flow For old, unhappy, far-off things And battles long ago ...
ANOTHER VOICE	The long day wanes: the slow moon climbs; the deep Moans round with many voices. Come, my friends, 'Tis not too late to seek a newer world ...
ANOTHER VOICE	I cannot praise a fugitive and cloister'd virtue, unexercised and unbreath'd, that never sallies out and sees her adversary ...
ANOTHER VOICE	Or ever the silver cord be loosed, or the golden bowl be broken ... Men must endure Their going hence, even as their coming hither: Ripeness is all ...
ANOTHER VOICE	The Lord is my Shepherd; I shall not want ...[1]
JOHNSON	(*Sitting, slowly and regretfully*) Ever since I saw you last, these many years, I think I have been foolish and ignorant, for you taught me long ago that in these voices, which come so quickly when we call on them, I would find wisdom and beauty. Though I remembered this, and sometimes, when business was not pressing and pleasure begain to pall, I heard echoes of the voices again, I did not ask them to give me their treasure. But I always felt there was a time

---

[1] The famous lines are from the following: Shakespeare *The Winter's Tale* IV:iii; Wordsworth *The Solitary Reaper*; Tennyson *Ulysses*; Milton *Areopagitica*; Ecclesiastes 12:6 (King James Bible); Shakespeare *King Lear* V:ii; Psalm 23:1 (King James Bible).

	ahead when at last I could sit by the fire and listen to them again; and now it seems there is no such time for me, only this brief last hour ...

MORRISON I doesn't matter, Robert. We don't know what Time is, let alone how it shall be divided for us. And this isn't the last frontier of Beauty. (*In brisker tone*) I'm glad to have seen you again, Robert.

JOHNSON (*A boy again, shyly*) And I you, sir. I always liked you the best, y'know, sir.

MORRISON (*Smiling*) If you hadn't I shouldn't have been here. Well – I must go.

Fighting Filth and Disease

from the stage play
An Enemy of the People   (1882)

by Henrik Ibsen

(translated from the Norwegian by Michael Meyer,
with some cuts for performance)

Ibsen was not only the most important theatrical figure of his generation: his plays changed the main character of European dramatic writing. He brought realism to the theatre – a realism that has lasted into many of the stage plays and most of the television plays and films of today. By bringing to the stage apparently real scenes from ordinary life, he explored deeper and wider universal human themes.

An Enemy of the People is set in a small, provincial town, actually in Norway but it could have been in any western country. The story grew in Ibsen's mind when a friend of his told him what had happened to his father. He was a doctor who discovered an outbreak of the serious disease cholera in the small spa town in which he lived, and which made its money out of visitors coming for the spa waters to help their health. He felt it his duty to make the outbreak of cholera public. He did this, but it ruined the season and therefore the income of the town. The local people stoned his house and forced him to flee the town with his family.

In the play, Dr Stockmann's job is medical officer at the Baths. He has been worried about various illnesses in residents and visitors during the last year, and he has had the water tested. He has just had confirmation that his investigations into the water have shown that it is unhealthy. Refuse from the leather tanneries has seeped into the water supply into the Baths and on to the well-regarded beaches. The water 'is definitely noxious to the health even for external use'.

Stockmann thinks that the discovery will be used by the town council to re-lay the pipe system and put the matter right. He thinks that people will be grateful for his discovery as it will avoid the risk of ill-health. The editor of the local newspaper, Hovstad, and the Chairman of the Property Owners' Association congratulate him and promise support. Will others do so also?

Earlier in the play his daughter, Petra, who is a teacher, says: 'There's so much fear of the truth everywhere! At home and at school. Here we've got to keep our mouths shut, and at school we have to stand up and tell lies to the children.' Soon after, his brother Peter, the Mayor (who is officially his employer), calls. He has read Stockmann's report.

Characters

DR THOMAS STOCKMANN, Medical Officer at the Baths
MRS CATHERINE STOCKMANN, his wife
PETRA, their daughter, a schoolteacher
MAYOR, Peter Stockmann, the doctor's elder brother

DR S (*Goes over to the dining-room and looks in*) Catherine – ! Oh, hallo, Petra, are you here?
PETRA (*Enters*) Yes, I've just got back from school.
MRS S (*Enters*) Hasn't he come yet?
DR S Peter? No. But I've been having a long talk with Hovstad. He's quite excited about this discovery of mine. It seems it has a much wider significance than I'd supposed. So he's placed his newspaper at my disposal, if I should need it.
MRS S But do you think you will?

DR S Oh no, I'm sure I won't. But it's good to know that one has the free press on one's side – the mouthpiece of liberal opinion. And what do you think? I've had a visit from the Chairman of the Property Owners' Association!

MRS S Oh? And what did he want?

DR S He's going to support me too. They're all going to support me, if there's any trouble. Catherine, do you know what I have behind me?

MRS S Behind you? No, what have you behind you?

DR S The solid majority.

MRS S I see. And that's a good thing, is it?

DR S Of course it's a good thing! (*Rubs his hands and walks up and down*) How splendid to feel that one stands shoulder to shoulder with one's fellow citizens in brotherly concord!

PETRA And that one's doing so much that's good and useful, father.

DR S Yes, and for one's home town too!

MRS S There's the doorbell.

DR S Ah, this must be him! (*A knock on the inner door*) Come in!

MAYOR (*Enters from the hall*) Good morning.

DR S (*Warmly*) Hallo, Peter!

MRS S Good morning, brother-in-law. How are you?

MAYOR Oh, thank you; so-so. (*To the* DOCTOR) Last night, after office hours, I received a thesis from you regarding the state of the water at the Baths.

DR S Yes. Have you read it?

MAYOR I have.

DR S Well! What do you think?

MAYOR (*Glances at the others*) Hm—

MRS S Come, Petra.

She and PETRA *go into the room on the left.*

FIGHTING FILTH AND DISEASE

MAYOR (*After a pause*) Was it necessary to conduct all these investigations behind my back?

DR S Well, until I was absolutely certain, I—

MAYOR And now you are?

DR S Yes. Surely you must be convinced—?

MAYOR Is it your intention to place this document before the Baths Committee as an official statement?

DR S Of course! Something must be done. And quickly.

MAYOR I find your phraseology in this document, as usual, somewhat extravagant. Amongst other things, you say that all we have to offer our visitors at present is a permanent state of ill-health.

DR S Peter, how else can you describe it? Just think! That water's poisonous even if you bathe in it, let alone drink it! And we're offering this to unfortunate people who are ill and who have turned to us in good faith, and are paying us good money, in order to get their health back!

MAYOR And your conclusion is that we must build a sewer to drain away these aforesaid impurities from the swamp at Moellerdal, and that the whole water system must be relaid.

DR S Can you think of any other solution? I can't.

MAYOR This morning I called upon the town engineer. In the course of our discussion I half jokingly mentioned these proposals as a thing we might possibly undertake some time in the future.

DR S Some time in the future?

MAYOR He smiled at what he obviously regarded as my extravagance – as I knew he would. Have you ever troubled to consider what these alterations you suggest would cost? According to the information I received, the expense would probably run into several hundred thousand crowns.

DR S Would it be that much?

MAYOR Yes. But that's not the worst. The work would take at least two years.

DR S Two years, did you say? Two whole years?

MAYOR At least. And what do we do with the Baths in the meantime? Close them? Yes, we'd be forced to. You don't imagine anyone would come here once the rumour got around that the water was impure?

DR S But, Peter, it is!

MAYOR There are other towns around with qualifications to be regarded as health resorts. Do you think they won't start trying to attract the market? Of course they will! And there we shall be! We'll probably have to abandon the whole expensive scheme, and you will have ruined the town.

DR S I – ruined—!

MAYOR It's only as a health resort – a Spa – that this town has any future worth speaking of. Surely you realise that as well as I do.

DR S But what do you propose we do?

MAYOR Your report has not completely convinced me that the situation is as dangerous as you imply.

DR S Oh, Peter, if anything it's worse! Or at least it will be in the summer, once the hot weather starts.

MAYOR As I said, I believe that you are exaggerating the danger. The existing water system at the Baths is a fact, and must be accepted as such. However, in due course I dare say the Committee might not be inflexibly opposed to considering whether, without unreasonable pecuniary sacrifice, it might not be possible to introduce certain improvements.

DR S And you think I'd lend my name to such chicanery?

MAYOR Chicanery!

DR S That's what it would be! A fraud, a lie, a crime against the community, against the whole of society!

MAYOR As I have already pointed out, I have not succeeded

in convincing myself that any immediate or critical danger exists.

DR S Oh, yes you have! But you won't admit it, because it was you who forced through the proposal that the Baths and the water pipes should be sited where they are, and you refuse to admit that you made a gross blunder. Don't be such a fool, do you think I don't see through you?

MAYOR And suppose you were right? If I do guard my reputation with a certain anxiety, it is because I have the welfare of our town at heart. Without moral authority I cannot guide and direct affairs as I deem most fit for the general good. For this, and diverse other reasons, it is vital to me that your report should not be placed before the Baths Committee. It must be suppressed for the general good. At a later date I shall bring the matter up for discussion, and we shall discreetly do the best we can. But nothing, not a single word, about this unfortunate matter must come to the public ear.

DR S Well, it can't be stopped now, my dear Peter.

MAYOR It must and shall be stopped.

DR S It can't, I tell you. Too many people know.

MAYOR Know? Who knows? You don't mean those fellows from the *People's Tribune*—?

DR S The free press of our country will see to it that you do your duty.

MAYOR (*After a short pause*) You're an exceedingly foolish man, Thomas. Haven't you considered what the consequences of this action may be for you?

DR S Consequences? Consequences for me?

MAYOR Yes. For you and for your family.

DR S What the devil do you mean by that?

MAYOR I think I have always shown myself a good brother to you, whenever you've needed help.

DR S You have, and I thank you for it.

MAYOR I'm not asking for thanks. To a certain extent I've been forced to do it – for my own sake. It's painful for a public servant to see his next-of-kin spend his entire time compromising himself.

DR S And you think I do that?

MAYOR Unfortunately you do, without knowing it. You have a restless, combative, rebellious nature. And then you've this unfortunate passion for rushing into print upon every possible – and impossible – subject. The moment you get an idea you have to sit down and write a newspaper article or a whole pamphlet about it.

DR S Surely if a man gets hold of a new idea it's his duty as a citizen to tell it to the public?

MAYOR People don't want new ideas. They're best served by the good old accepted ideas they have already.

DR S And you can say that to my face!

MAYOR Oh, Thomas, you're impossible to work with. You never consider anyone else's feelings. You even seem to forget it's me you have to thank for getting you your job at the Baths—

DR S It was mine by right! I was the first person to see that this town could become a flourishing watering place! For many years I fought alone for this idea! I wrote, and wrote—

MAYOR No one denies that. But the time wasn't ripe then. But as soon as the right moment arrived, I – and others – took the matter up—

DR S Yes, and made a mess of my wonderful plan! Oh yes, it's becoming very clear now what brilliant fellows you were!

MAYOR As far as I can see, all you're looking for now is just another excuse for a fight. You've always got to pick a quarrel with your superiors – it's your old failing. You can't bear to have anyone in authority over you. But now I've shown you what's at stake, for the whole town, and for myself too. And I'm not prepared to compromise.

DR S What do you mean?

MAYOR Since you have been so indiscreet as to discuss this delicate matter, which you ought to have kept a professional secret, the affair obviously cannot be hushed up. All kinds of rumours will spread around, and the malicious elements among us will feed these rumours with details of their own invention. It is therefore necessary that you publicly deny these rumours.

DR S I don't understand you.

MAYOR I feel sure that on further investigation you will convince yourself that the situation is not nearly as critical as you had at first supposed.

DR S Aha; you feel sure, do you?

MAYOR I also feel sure you will publicly express your confidence that the Committee will remedy any possible defects which may exist.

DR S But you can't remedy the defect by just patching things up! I'm telling you, Peter, unless you start again from scratch, it's my absolute conviction that—

MAYOR As an employee you have no right to any independent conviction.

DR S (*Starts*) No right!

MAYOR As an employee. As a private person – well, heaven knows that's another matter. But as a subordinate official at the Baths, you have no right to express any opinion which conflicts with that of your superiors.

DR S This is going too far! I, a doctor, a man of science, have no right—!

MAYOR The question is not merely one of science. The issues involved are both technical and economical.

DR S I don't care how you define the bloody thing! I must be free to say what I think about anything!

MAYOR Go ahead. As long as it isn't anything connected with the Baths. That we forbid you.

DR S (*Shouts*) You forbid—! You—! Why, you're just a—

MAYOR *I* forbid you – I, your chief! And when I forbid you to do something, you must obey!

DR S (*Controls himself*) Peter – if you weren't my brother—!

PETRA (*Throws open the door*) Father, don't put up with this!

MRS S (*Follows her*) Petra, Petra!

MAYOR Ha! Eavesdroppers!

MRS S You were talking so loud – we couldn't help hearing—

PETRA I was listening.

MAYOR Well. I'm not altogether sorry—

DR S (*Goes closer to him*) You spoke to me of forbidding and obeying?

MAYOR You forced me to use that tone.

DR S And you expect me to publicly swallow my own words?

MAYOR We regard it as an unavoidable necessity that you issue a statement on the lines I have indicated.

DR S And if I don't – obey?

MAYOR Then we shall be forced to issue an explanation, to calm the public.

DR S All right! But I shall write and refute you. I stick to my views. I shall prove that I am right and you are wrong. And what will you do then?

MAYOR Then I shall be unable to prevent your dismissal.

DR S What—!

PETRA Father! Dismissal!

MRS S Dismissal!

MAYOR Dismissal from your post as public medical officer. I shall feel compelled to apply for immediate notice to be served on you, barring you from any further connection with the Baths.

DR S You'd have the impudence to do that?

MAYOR You're the one who's being impudent.

PETRA Uncle, this is a disgraceful way to treat a man like father!

MRS S Be quiet, Petra.

MAYOR (*Looks at* PETRA) So we've opinions of our own already, have we? But of course! (*To* MRS STOCKMANN) Sister-in-law, you seem to be the most sensible person in this house. Use what influence you have over your husband. Make him realise the consequences this will have both for his family and—

DR S My family concerns no one but myself.

MAYOR —both for his family, and for the town he lives in.

DR S I'm the one who has the town's real interests at heart! I want to expose the evils that sooner or later must come to light. I'm going to prove to people that I love this town where I was born.

MAYOR Oh, you're blind! All you're trying to do is to stop up the source of the town's prosperity.

DR S That source is poisoned, man! Are you mad? We live by hawking filth and disease! And all this communal life you boast so much about is based upon a lie!

MAYOR That's pure imagination – if nothing worse. The man who casts such foul aspersions against the town he lives in is an enemy of society.

DR S (*Goes towards him*) You dare to—!

MRS S (*Throws herself between them*) Thomas!

PETRA (*Grasps her father by the arm*) Keep calm, father!

MAYOR I shall not expose myself to violence. You've been warned. Consider what is your duty to yourself and your family. Goodbye. (*Goes*)

DR S (*Walks up and down*) And in my own house too, Catherine!

MRS S Yes, Thomas. It's a shame and a scandal—
PETRA I'd like to get my hands on him—!
DR S It's my own fault. I ought to have exposed them long ago! I should have bared my teeth; and used them! Calling me an enemy of society! By God, I'm not going to take that lying down!
MRS S But, Thomas dear, might is right—
DR S I'm the one who's right!
MRS S What's the good of being right if you don't have the might?
PETRA Mother, how can you speak like that?
DR S (*Laughs*) Oh, Catherine, just give me time. You'll see! I'm going to fight this war to the end.
MRS S Yes, and the end will be that you'll lose your job. What about your family, Thomas?
PETRA Oh, mother, don't always think only of us.
MRS S It's easy for you to talk. You can stand on your own feet, if need be. But think of the boys, Thomas! Look at them! What's to become of them?

EILIF *and* MORTEN *have meanwhile entered, carrying their schoolbooks.*

DR S My sons! (*Suddenly stands erect, his mind made up*) Even if my whole world crashes about me, I shall never bow my head. (*Goes towards his room*)
MRS S Thomas, what are you going to do?
DR S (*In the doorway*) I want to have the right to look my sons in the eyes when they grow up into free men! (*Goes into his room*)
MRS S Oh, God help us!

The Mystery of Goodness

from the libretto for the opera
Billy Budd by Benjamin Britten   (1951)

by E. M. Forster and Eric Crozier

(based on the short novel by Herman Melville,
written 1891)

The opera takes place at sea during the English–French wars of 1797. The main characters come together for the climax of the story in this, the last full scene of the opera.

In this war, the English navy 'press-ganged' ordinary Englishmen, that is, captured them and forced them to join the navy. One is the young Billy Budd, who is seized and put aboard the warship HMS *Indomitable*. Billy is an orphan. He has a very bad stutter, which makes it difficult for him to communicate at important moments. He looks forward to his new life on board, and is determined to be a good seaman. He greatly admires the captain of the ship, Vere. Billy becomes popular with the other sailors, one singing: 'He's a good cuss is Billy!' However, the Master-at-Arms, Claggart, is a really evil man, who admires Billy and is torn between wanting to help him and to destroy him. (The square brackets in the extract indicate that in the opera those lines are sung at the same time. In reading, it is suggested that they should be spoken in the order printed.)

Characters

JOHN CLAGGART, Master-at-Arms
CAPTAIN VERE, Commander of the *Indomitable*
BILLY BUDD, able seaman

FIRST LIEUTENANT, Mr Redburn
SAILING MASTER
MR RATCLIFFE, second lieutenant
DANSKER, an old seaman
sailors as QUARTER-DECK CHORUS

The deck is silent and dark. CLAGGART *stands alone in the small pool of light by the companion-way.*

CLAGGART O beauty, O handsomeness, goodness! Would that I never encountered you! Would that I lived in my own world always, in that depravity to which I was born. There I found peace of a sort, there I established an order such as reigns in Hell. But alas, alas! the light shines in the darkness, and the darkness comprehends it and suffers. O beauty, O handsomeness, goodness! would that I had never seen you!

Having seen you, what choice remains to me? None, none! I am doomed to annihilate you, I am vowed to your destruction. I will wipe you off the face of the earth, off this tiny floating fragment of earth, off this ship where fortune has led you. First I will trouble your happiness. I will mutilate and silence the body where you dwell. It shall hang from the yard-arm, it shall fall into the depths of the sea, and all shall be as if nothing had been. No, you cannot escape! With hate and envy I am stronger than love.

So may it be! O beauty, O handsomeness, goodness! you are surely in my power tonight. Nothing can defend you. Nothing! So may it be! For what hope remains if love can escape?

If love still lives and grows strong where I cannot enter, what hope is there in my own dark world for me? No! I cannot believe it! That were torment too keen.

> I, John Claggart, Master-at-Arms upon the *Indomitable*, have you in my power, and I will destroy you.

Claggart accuses Billy of being on the side of the enemy and planning to mutiny. Billy is brought before Captain Vere, who senses that he is an unusually good person, but has to listen to the case.

Scene 2

The Captain's cabin. VERE *is alone.*

VERE Claggart, John Claggart, beware! I'm not so easily deceived. The boy whom you would destroy, he is good; you are evil. You have reckoned without me. I have studied men and their ways. The mists are vanishing – and you shall fail!

He goes to the door and opens it. BILLY *enters.*

BILLY (*Radiant*) You wanted to see me. I knew it, I knew I'd be called. Captain of the mizzen![1] Oh, the honour! – and you telling me! I shouldn't speak so quick, but the talk's got around.

VERE (*Watching him*) Would you like to be captain of the mizzen, Billy Budd?

BILLY Yes, or to be your coxswain. I'd like that too.

VERE Why?

BILLY To be near you. I'd serve you well, indeed I would. You'd be safe with me. You could trust your boat to me. Couldn't find a better coxswain – that's to say, I'll look after you my best. I'd die for you – so would they all.

Aren't I glad to be here! Didn't know what life was

---

[1] the team of sailors responsible for the sails and rigging on 'the mizzen mast', the third one

before now, and O for a fight! Wish we'd got that Frenchie I do, but we'll catch her another day. Sir! let me be your coxswain! I'd look after you well. You could trust your boat to me, you'd be safe with me. Please, sir!

VERE (*Aside*) And this is the man I'm told is dangerous – the schemer, the plotter, the artful mutineer! This is the trap concealed in the daisies! Claggart, John Claggart, beware! (*To* BILLY) You must forget all that for the present. I do not want to see you about promotion.

BILLY (*Good humoured*) That's all right, sir. I'm content.

VERE Very well, but now listen to me, Budd. We want to question you – I and the Master-at-Arms.

BILLY Yes, sir!

VERE Answer us frankly and show all proper respect. Now stand to attention. (*He calls*) Boy! Admit Mr Claggart.

The door opens. CLAGGART *enters.*

Master-at-Arms and foretopman, I speak to you both. You stand before your Commander as accuser and accused under the Articles of War. Remember both of you the penalties of falsehood. Master-at-Arms, stand there. Tell this man to his face what you have already told me.

CLAGGART (*Staring at* BILLY) William Budd, I accuse you of insubordination and disaffection.

William Budd, I accuse you of aiding our enemies and spreading their infamous creed of 'The Rights of Man'.[2]

William Budd, I accuse you of bringing French gold on board to bribe your comrades and lure them from their duty.

---

[2] a book (by Thomas Paine) supporting the revolution in France

> William Budd, you are a traitor to your country and to your King.
>
> I accuse you of mutiny!

VERE William Budd, answer. Defend yourself!
BILLY (*Unable to speak*) ..a..a..a..a..a.
VERE Speak, man, speak.
BILLY ..a..a..a..a..a.
VERE Take your time, my boy, take your time.

VERE lays his hand on BILLY's shoulder. BILLY's right fist shoots out, striking CLAGGART on the forehead.

BILLY ..a..a..a...DEVIL!

CLAGGART falls and, after a couple of gasps, lies motionless.

VERE God o'mercy! (*He kneels by the corpse*) Here, help me!

BILLY does not move. VERE raises the body. It falls back.

> He's dead. Fated boy, what have you done? Go in there. Go! God help us! help us all.

BILLY obeys VERE and goes into a small stateroom at the back of the cabin. VERE goes to the door and calls to the BOY.

> Boy! fetch my officers at once.
>
> The mists have cleared. O terror! what do I see? Scylla and Charybdis,[3] the straits of Hell. I sight them too late – I see all the mists concealed. Beauty, handsomeness, goodness coming to trial. How can I condemn him? How can I save him? My heart's broken, my life's broken. It is not his trial, it is mine, mine. It is I whom the devil awaits.

---

[3] a dangerous rock and whirlpool respectively, with a narrow passage in between, so that a boat risked being destroyed by one if the sailors tried to avoid the other

The 1ST LIEUTENANT, SAILING MASTER *and* RATCLIFFE *enter the cabin hurriedly.*

Gentlemen, William Budd here has killed the Master-at-Arms.

1ST LIEUT, S MASTER AND RATCLIFFE
Great God! for what reason?

1ST LIEUT	We must keep our heads.
S MASTER	Oh! what unheard-of brutality.
RATCLIFFE	The boy has been provoked.

1ST LIEUT	Why did he do it? What is the truth?
S MASTER	Claggart is lost to us – we must revenge him.
RATCLIFFE	There's no harm in the boy. I cannot believe it.

1ST LIEUT	Justice is our duty, justice is our hope.
S MASTER	Claggart, he's dead – give the murderer the rope.
RATCLIFFE	Mercy on his youth – there's no harm in the lad.

1ST LIEUT	Here and now we'll judge the case.
S MASTER	Neither Heaven nor Hell suffer villainy to rest.
RATCLIFFE	Heaven is merciful – let us be merciful.

1ST LIEUT	Call him to trial!
S MASTER	We must have revenge, revenge!
RATCLIFFE	Let us show pity, show pity!
VERE	Struck by an angel of God. Yet the angel must hang.

1ST LIEUT	Sir, command us.
S MASTER	Unheard-of in naval annals.
RATCLIFFE	What's to be done?

VERE Justice must be done. I summon a drum-head court.[4] The enemy is near. The prisoner must be tried at once. Mr Redburn presides. I myself am present as

---

[4] a court quickly called round a drum on a battlefield to decide what to do with an offender

witness – the sole earthly witness. Gentlemen, the court sits.

The Officers prepare the cabin for the court-martial. VERE *stands rigidly at the side. They carry the body into another stateroom, set table and chairs, and then summon* BILLY *before them.*

1ST LIEUT William Budd, you are accused by Captain Vere of striking your superior officer, John Claggart, Master-at-Arms, and thus causing his death.

BILLY *is silent.*

1ST LIEUT Captain Vere?
VERE The Master-at-Arms ... denounced the prisoner to me ... for spreading disaffection ... sympathy with our enemies ... and trying to start a mutiny ...
BILLY No, no!
VERE ... having French gold for bribes. I asked the prisoner to reply. He stammered, then struck out, struck John Claggart on the forehead, and the rest you know.
1ST LIEUT (*To* BILLY) Captain Vere has spoken. Is it as he has said?
BILLY Yes.
1ST LIEUT You know the Articles of War?
BILLY Yes.
1ST LIEUT And the penalty?
BILLY Yes.
1ST LIEUT Why did you do it?
BILLY Sir, I am loyal to my country and my King. It is true I am a nobody, who don't know where he was born, and I've had to live rough, but never, never could I do those foul things. It's a lie.
1ST LIEUT Did you bear any malice against the Master-at-Arms?
BILLY No, no I tried to answer him back. My tongue

	wouldn't work, so I had to say it with a blow, and it killed him.
1ST LIEUT	You stammered then?
BILLY	Ay, it comes and goes.
1ST LIEUT	Why should the Master-at-Arms accuse you wrongfully? Why?
BILLY	Don't know, don't know such things. Ask Captain Vere. Ask him.
1ST LIEUT	Do you, sir, know any reason?
VERE	I have told you all I have seen. I have no more to say.
1ST LIEUT	Prisoner, have you any more to say?
BILLY	Captain Vere, save me!
1ST LIEUT	Go in and wait.
BILLY	Captain, save me!
1ST LIEUT	Go in.
BILLY	I'd have died for you, save me!
1ST LIEUT	Go in.
BILLY	Save me!

The other officers lead BILLY *back to the small stateroom.*

1ST LIEUT	Poor fellow, who could save him?
S MASTER	Ay, he must swing.
RATCLIFFE	Ay, there's naught to discuss.
TOGETHER	We've no choice.
1ST LIEUT	There's the Mutiny Act.
S MASTER	There are the Articles of War.
RATCLIFFE	There are the King's Regulations.
TOGETHER	We've no choice.
1ST LIEUT	Claggart I never liked. Still, he did his duty.
S MASTER	No one liked Claggart. Still, he's been murdered.
RATCLIFFE	Claggart was hard on them all. How they hated him.
TOGETHER	We've no choice.

THE MYSTERY OF GOODNESS

1ST LIEUT ⎫ Baby Budd the men called him. They loved him.
S MASTER ⎬ Billy Budd! He might have been a leader.
RATCLIFFE ⎭ Billy Budd – I impressed him[5] – King's bargain.

TOGETHER But we've no choice.

1ST LIEUT What, then, is our verdict?

OFFICERS (*To* VERE) Sir, before we decide, join us, help us with your knowledge and wisdom. Grant us your guidance.

VERE No. Do not ask me. I cannot.

OFFICERS Sir, we need you as always.

VERE No. Pronounce your verdict.

OFFICERS Guilty.

VERE And the penalty?

OFFICERS Death.

1ST LIEUT Hanging from the yard-arm.

VERE I accept your verdict. Let the Master-at-Arms be buried with full naval honours. All hands to witness punishment at one bell in the morning watch. I will myself tell the prisoner.

1ST LIEUT Gentlemen, the court rises.

The Officers salute and leave quietly.

VERE I accept their verdict. Death is the penalty for those who break the laws of earth. And I who am king of this fragment of earth, of this floating monarchy, have enacted death. But I have seen the divine judgement of Heaven, I've seen iniquity overthrown. Cooped in this narrow cabin I have beheld the mystery of goodness – and I am afraid.

Before what tribunal do I stand if I destroy goodness? The angel of God has struck and the angel must hang – through me. Beauty, handsomeness,

---

[5] press-ganged, that is captured to make him a sailor

goodness, it is for me to destroy you. I, Edward Fairfax Vere, Captain of the *Indomitable*, lost with all hands on the infinite sea. (*He goes towards the door of* BILLY's *stateroom*) I am the messenger of death! How can he pardon? How receive me?

He goes towards the small stateroom and enters it. The curtain remains up until the end of the music, and then slowly falls.

Scene 3

A bay of the gun-deck, shortly before dawn next morning. BILLY *is in irons between two cannon.*

BILLY   Look!
Through the port comes the moon-shine astray!
It tips the guard's cutlass and silvers this nook;
But 'twill die in the dawning of Billy's last day.
Ay, ay, all is up; and I must up too
Early in the morning, aloft from below.
On an empty stomach, now, never would it do.
They'll give me a nibble – bit of biscuit ere I go.
Sure a messmate will reach me the last parting cup;
But turning heads away from the hoist and the belay,
Heaven knows who will have the running of me up!
No pipe to those halyards – but ain't it all sham?
A blur's in my eyes; it is dreaming that I am.
But Donald he has promised to stand by the plank,
So I'll shake a friendly hand ere I sink.
But no! It is dead then I'll be, come to think.
They'll lash me in hammocks, drop me in deep,
Fathoms down, fathoms – how I'll dream fast asleep.

> I feel it stealing now...
>
> > Roll me over fair.
>
> I am sleepy, and the oozy weeds about me twist.

DANSKER *steals in with a mug of grog.*

DANSKER (*Whispering*) Here! Baby!

BILLY Dansker, old friend! that's kind. (*He drinks*) That's kind. Gimme a biscuit too – (*He eats*) – I feel better. But you shouldn't have risked coming to see me. You'll get into trouble.

DANSKER All's trouble. The whole ship's trouble ... and upside-down.

BILLY What for?

DANSKER Some reckon to rescue you, Billy Boy. How they hated that Jemmy Legs! They swear you shan't swing. They love you.

BILLY I'll swing and they'll swing. Tell 'em that and stop them. (*He puts the mug down*) Christ! I feel better. Done me a lot of good – a drink and seeing a friend. Stopped me from thinking on what's no use and dreaming what needn't be dreamt, and woken me up to face what must be. What's the day to be?

DANSKER A fair day.

BILLY We'd have caught that Frenchie on a fair day. O that cursèd mist! Maybe you'll still catch her. You better be going now.

DANSKER Goodbye, Baby.

BILLY (*Holding up his wrists*) Can't shake hands. Chaplain's been here before you – kind – and good his story, of the good boy hung and gone to glory, hung for the likes of me. But I had to strike down that Jemmy Legs – it's fate. And Captain Vere has had to strike me down – Fate. We are both in sore trouble, him and me, with great need for strength, and my trouble's soon ending, so I can't help him longer with his.

Starry Vere, God bless him – and the clouds darker than night for us both. Dansker of the *Indomitable*, help him all of you. Dansker, goodbye? (DANSKER *goes*) And farewell to ye, old *Rights o' Man*! Never your joys no more. Farewell to this grand rough world! Never more shipmates, no more sea, no looking down from the heights to the depths! But I've sighted a sail in the storm, the far-shining sail that's not Fate, and I'm contented. I've seen where she's bound for. She has a land of her own where she'll anchor for ever. Oh, I'm contented. Don't matter now being hanged, or being forgotten and caught in the weeds. Don't matter now. I'm strong, and I know it, and I'll stay strong, and that's all, and that's enough.

The curtain falls.

Scene 4

The main-deck and quarter-deck. Four o'clock the same morning, and first daylight is appearing. When the curtain rises the decks are empty, save for a few of the watch on duty and the Marine sentry. The whole crew assembles in silence and in perfect order. They arrive in the following groups:
Gunners.
Seamen.
Afterguardsmen.
Powder-monkeys[6] *(who run in and clamber up the rigging, and on to boats and booms).*
Marines (who march across to the quarter-deck).
Officers and Midshipmen – on the quarter-deck. VERE, *preceded by the* 1ST LIEUTENANT, SAILING MASTER *and* LIEUTENANT RATCLIFFE.

---

[6] young boys used to get the ship's cannons ready with gun-powder

When all are in position, BILLY *enters, preceded and followed by Marine sentries.*

1ST LIEUT (*Reading*) 'According to the Articles of War, it is provided as follows:

If any officer, mariner, soldier or other person in the fleet shall strike any of his superior officers, he shall suffer death.

It is further provided that if any in the fleet commits murder, he shall be punished by death.'

William Budd, you have been found by the court-martial guilty of striking your superior officer. You have further been found guilty of murder. In accordance with the aforesaid Articles of War, you are condemned to death by hanging from the yard-arm.

BILLY (*Suddenly*) Starry Vere, God bless you!

ALL VOICES (*except* VERE *and* BILLY) Starry Vere, God bless you!

The 1ST LIEUTENANT *closes his book. At this signal, the Marine sentries and* BILLY *turn about and march off towards the main-mast. All watch the scene off stage. The light of dawn has grown to a fresh pink.* CAPTAIN VERE *removes his hat. As he does so, all faces turn slowly upward to follow the body of* BILLY *to the main-yard. Then begins the sound described by Melville as like the freshet wave of a torrent roaring distantly through the woods, expressing a capricious revulsion of feeling in the crew. The sound grows and grows, and the whole wedged mass of faces slowly turns in rebellion to the quarter-deck. There is a growing agitation among the Officers on the quarter-deck, but* VERE *stands motionless.*

1ST LIEUT, S MASTER AND RATCLIFFE
Down all hands! And see that they go!

QUARTER-DECK CHORUS
>Down all hands! Down!

The men slowly obey the commands from force of habit and begin to disperse.

QUARTER-DECK CHORUS
>Down all hands! See that they go! Down!

The deck empties by degrees and the light slowly fades.

Death of a Martyr

from the verse play
Murder in the Cathedral   (1935)

by T. S. Eliot

Eight hundred years ago England was of course a very different country in most ways, but the conflict between Thomas Becket and King Henry II is similar to conflicts between people of religious faith and their rulers throughout the centuries. T. S. Eliot, one of the greatest poets of the twentieth century, wrote this play for performance in Canterbury Cathedral, where Becket was murdered, at the time when Communism and Fascism were taking control in a number of countries and denying individuals the right to religious beliefs. Becket is famous throughout the world for his struggle to keep the Catholic Church in England free from royal control.

Becket was born in about 1118 in Cheapside, in the City of London. He worked as a clerk, and the young king made him Chancellor of England in 1155. Becket enjoyed a luxurious lifestyle and became Henry's favourite companion. In 1162 Henry made him Archbishop of Canterbury, the senior position in the English Church. He took his new position very seriously, lived more simply, and became a champion of the Church against royal power.

This led to many serious and bitter conflicts between the king and the archbishop, and Becket fled to France, fearing for his life. Six years later, in December 1170, Becket returned to Canterbury and continued his opposition to the king. A later story says that Henry made an angry remark about Becket in the presence of his knights: 'Will no one rid me of this turbulent priest?' Four knights took this as a royal request and went to Canterbury, though they may not at first have meant to kill Becket.

Eliot's play has a chorus of women of Canterbury who chant about the situation, analyse it, and as in other plays from Japan to Ireland are the voice of humanity commenting on what is happening. In the first half of the play the scene is set, and Thomas Becket is tempted in various ways by spiritual tempters who appear in his mind. The first tries to seduce him back to the rich carefree life of his time at court; the second makes him think of worldly power and whether he would like to go back to being Chancellor; the third suggests joining with the lords to create a new power-base. Then there is an unexpected fourth tempter. He advises Thomas to 'think of glory after death ... Saint and Martyr rule from the tomb':

> Think, Thomas, think of enemies dismayed,
> Creeping in penance, frightened of a shade;
> Think of pilgrims, standing in line
> Before the glittering jewelled shrine,
> From generation to generation
> Bending the knees in supplication,
> Think of the miracles, by God's grace,
> And think of your enemies in another place.

In other words, it is tempting to Thomas to try to become a martyr, and to know that he will live for ever in people's memories. He fights that very persuasive temptation. As he says in a soliloquy:

> Now is my way clear, now is the meaning plain;
> Temptation shall not come in this kind again.
> The last temptation is the greatest treason:
> To do the right deed for the wrong reason.

Then Thomas finds the answer to this fourth temptation: 'the true martyr is he who has become the instrument of God, who has lost his will in the will of God, and who no longer desires anything for himself, not even the glory of being a martyr'.

In this extract, the scene is Canterbury Cathedral, 29 December 1170. The knights are armed and looking for Thomas; the priests drag him into the cathedral where they think he will be safe.

Characters

THOMAS BECKET, Archbishop of Canterbury
THREE PRIESTS, of Canterbury Cathedral
FOUR KNIGHTS
CHORUS, of women of Canterbury

In the cathedral. THOMAS *and* PRIESTS.

PRIESTS Bar the door. Bar the door.
The door is barred.
We are safe. We are safe.
They dare not break in.
They cannot break in. They have not the force.
We are safe. We are safe.

THOMAS Unbar the doors! throw open the doors!
I will not have the house of prayer, the church of Christ,
The sanctuary, turned into a fortress.
The Church shall protect her own, in her own way, not
As oak and stone; stone and oak decay,
Give no stay, but the Church shall endure.
The church shall be open, even to our enemies.
    Open the door!

1ST PRIEST My Lord! these are not men, these come not as men come, but
Like maddened beasts. They come not like men, who
Respect the sanctuary, who kneel to the Body of Christ,
But like beasts. You would bar the door
Against the lion, the leopard, the wolf or the boar,
Why not more
Against beasts with the souls of damned men, against men
Who would damn themselves to beasts. My Lord! My Lord!

THOMAS Unbar the door!
You think me reckless, desperate and mad.
You argue by results, as this world does,
To settle if an act be good or bad.
You defer to the fact. For every life and every act
Consequence of good and evil can be shown.
And as in time results of many deeds are blended
So good and evil in the end become confounded.
It is not in time that my death shall be known;
It is out of time that my decision is taken
If you call that decision
To which my whole being gives entire consent.
I give my life
To the Law of God above the Law of Man.
Unbar the door! unbar the door!
We are not here to triumph by fighting, by stratagem, or by resistance,
Not to fight with beasts as men. We have fought the beast
And have conquered. We have only to conquer
Now, by suffering. This is the easier victory.
Now is the triumph of the Cross, now
Open the door! I command it. OPEN THE DOOR!

DEATH OF A MARTYR

The door is opened. The KNIGHTS *enter, slightly tipsy.*

PRIESTS This way, my Lord! Quick. Up the stair. To the roof.
To the crypt. Quick. Come. Force him.

KNIGHTS Where is Becket, the traitor to the King?
    Where is Becket, the meddling priest?
Come down Daniel to the lions' den,
    Come down Daniel for the mark of the beast.

Are you washed in the blood of the Lamb?
    Are you marked with the mark of the beast?
Come down Daniel to the lions' den,
    Come down Daniel and join in the feast.

Where is Becket the Cheapside brat?
    Where is Becket the faithless priest?
Come down Daniel to the lions' den,
    Come down Daniel and join in the feast.

THOMAS It is the just man who
Like a bold lion, should be without fear.
I am here.
No traitor to the King. I am a priest,
A Christian, saved by the blood of Christ,
Ready to suffer with my blood.
This is the sign of the Church always,
The sign of blood. Blood for blood.
His blood given to buy my life,
My blood given to pay for his death,
My death for His death.

1ST KNIGHT Absolve all those you have excommunicated.[1]

2ND KNIGHT Resign the powers you have arrogated.

3RD KNIGHT Restore to the King the money you appropriated.

1ST KNIGHT Renew the obedience you have violated.

THOMAS For my Lord I am now ready to die,

---

[1] In the Catholic Church, to excommunicate someone is to cut them off from any future life in the Church. It is the extreme punishment.

	That his Church may have peace and liberty.
	Do with me as you will, to your hurt and shame;
	But none of my people, in God's name,
	Whether layman or clerk, shall you touch.
	This I forbid.
KNIGHTS	Traitor! traitor! traitor!
THOMAS	You, Reginald, three times traitor you:
	Traitor to me as my temporal vassal,
	Traitor to me as your spiritual lord,
	Traitor to God in desecrating His Church.
1ST KNIGHT	No faith do I owe to a renegade,
	And what I owe shall now be paid.

THOMAS Now to Almighty God, to the Blessed Mary ever Virgin, to the blessed John the Baptist, the holy apostles Peter and Paul, to the blessed martyr Denys, and to all the Saints, I commend my cause and that of the Church.

While the KNIGHTS *kill him, we hear the* CHORUS.

CHORUS Clear the air! clean the sky! wash the wind! take stone from stone and wash them.
The land is foul, the water is foul, our beasts and ourselves defiled with blood.
A rain of blood has blinded my eyes. Where is England? where is Kent? where is Canterbury?
O far far far far in the past; and I wander in a land of barren boughs: if I break them, they bleed; I wander in a land of dry stones: if I touch them they bleed.
How how can I ever return, to the soft quiet seasons?
Night stay with us, stop sun, hold season, let the day not come, let the spring not come.
Can I look again at the day and its common things, and see them all smeared with blood, through a curtain of falling blood?

Talk More Genteel

from the musical *My Fair Lady* (1956)

by Alan Jay Lerner

(with music by Frederick Loewe, based on the play
Pygmalion (1913) by George Bernard Shaw)

Shaw was already a successful writer of plays when he had the idea for *Pygmalion*. The title is drawn from a Greek myth in which a sculptor called Pygmalion so adored a statue of a beautiful woman he had created that he prayed to the goddess of love to breathe life into his statue. The goddess answered his prayer.

Shaw was very interested in the English language, and how badly it was taught and how difficult its spelling makes pronunciation. He declared: 'It is impossible for an Englishman to open his mouth without making some other Englishman despise him.'

In the play and the musical based on it, late one rainy summer's night in London's Covent Garden, a man is seen making notes as he listens to the people around him speaking. He is suspected of being some sort of policeman searching out trouble. The people in the crowd turn against him. But it becomes clear that he is interested only in *how* they talk, and that he can tell from how each person speaks what part of London she or he was brought up in. He says: 'You can spot an Irishman or a Yorkshireman by his brogue. *I* can place any man within six miles. I can place him within two miles in London.' He is a professor of phonetics, Henry Higgins.

He becomes fascinated by the very strong Lisson Grove accent of a flower-seller, and carefully notes down a long drawn-out sound of amazement she makes: 'Ah-ah-ah-Ow-ow-ow-oo!' It leads him to declare:

> You see this creature with her kerbstone English; the English that will keep her in the gutter to the end of her days? Well, sir, in six months I could pass her off as a duchess at an Embassy ball. I could even get her a place as a lady's maid or shop assistant, which requires better English.

Unexpectedly, she takes up the idea and with the money she collected that night, turns up at his study the next morning to ask for lessons. Henry Higgins is meeting an Indian army officer, Colonel Pickering, who is an expert on the Indian language Sanskrit. Higgins is showing Pickering his recording machinery, and explaining how he studies accents. Eventually, he agrees to work on Eliza Doolittle's accent and make people accept her as an educated lady. Shaw himself said of what happened in the play:

> For the encouragement of people troubled with accents that cut them off from all high employment, I may add that the change wrought by Professor Higgins in the flower girl is neither impossible nor uncommon.

Characters

PROFESSOR HIGGINS
COLONEL PICKERING
MRS PEARCE, Higgins' housekeeper
ELIZA DOOLITTLE, the flower girl

Higgins' study: a room on the first floor. The room is in darkness. Sounds are coming from a loudspeaker.

TALK MORE GENTEEL

PICKERING I say, Higgins, couldn't we turn on the lights?

HIGGINS Nonsense, you hear much better in the dark.

PICKERING But it's a fearful strain listening to all these vowel sounds. I'm quite done up for this morning.

MRS PEARCE enters. She is HIGGINS' housekeeper.

MRS PEARCE Mr Higgins, are you there?

HIGGINS What is it, Mrs Pearce? (*He turns down the volume of the machine*)

MRS PEARCE A young woman wants to see you, sir.

HIGGINS (*Turning the machine off*) A young woman! What does she want? (*He switches on the light*) Has she an interesting accent? (*To* PICKERING) Let's have her up. Show her up, Mrs Pearce.

MRS PEARCE Very well, sir. It's for you to say. (*She goes out into the hall*)

HIGGINS This is rather a bit of luck. I'll show you how I make records. We'll set her talking; and I'll take her down in Bell's Visible Speech; then in Broad Romic[1]; and then we'll get her on the phonograph so that you can turn her on as often as you like with the written transcript before you.

MRS PEARCE (*Returning*) This is the young woman, sir.

ELIZA enters in state. She has a hat with three ostrich feathers, orange, sky-blue and red. She has a nearly clean apron, and the shoddy coat has been tidied a little. The pathos of this deplorable figure, with its innocent vanity and consequential air, touches PICKERING, *who has already straightened himself in the presence of* MRS PEARCE. *But as to* HIGGINS, *the only distinction he makes between men and women is that when he is neither bullying nor exclaiming to the heavens against some featherweight cross, he coaxes*

---

[1] a script for noting pronunciation patterns

women as a child coaxes its nurse when it wants to get anything out of her.

HIGGINS (*Brusquely, recognising her with unconcealed disappointment, and at once, babylike, making an intolerable grievance of it*) Why, this is the girl I jotted down last night. She's no use: I've got all the records I want of the Lisson Grove lingo,[2] and I'm not going to waste another cylinder on it. (*To the girl*) Be off with you: I don't want you.

ELIZA Don't be so saucy. You ain't heard what I come for yet. (*To* MRS PEARCE, *who is waiting at the door for further instructions*) Did you tell him I come in a taxi?

MRS PEARCE Nonsense, girl! What do you think a gentleman like Mr Higgins cares what you came in?

ELIZA Oh, we are proud! He ain't above giving lessons, not him: I heard him say so. Well, I ain't come here to ask for any compliment; and if my money's not good enough I can go elsewhere.

HIGGINS Good enough for what?

ELIZA Good enough for ye-oo. Now you know, don't you? I'm come to have lessons, I am. And to pay for 'em too: make no mistake.

HIGGINS (*Stunned*) Well!!! (*Recovering his breath with a gasp*) What do you expect me to say to you?

ELIZA Well, if you was a gentleman, you might ask me to sit down, I think. Don't I tell you I'm bringing you business?

HIGGINS Pickering, shall we ask this baggage to sit down, or shall we throw her out of the window?

ELIZA (*Running away in terror*) Ah-ah-oh-ow-ow-ow-oo! (*Wounded and whimpering*) I won't be called a baggage when I've offered to pay like any lady!

PICKERING (*Gently*) What is it you want, my girl?

---

[2] the way of speaking that was usual in the Lisson Grove part of north-west London

ELIZA I want to be a lady in a flower shop, 'stead of selling at the corner of Tottenham Court Road. But they won't take me unless I can talk more genteel. He said he could teach me. Well, here I am ready to pay him – not asking any favour – and he treats me as if I was dirt. I know what lessons cost as well as you do; and I'm ready to pay.

HIGGINS How much?

ELIZA (*Coming back to him, triumphant*) Now you're talking! I thought you'd come off it when you saw a chance of getting back a bit of what you chucked at me last night. (*Confidentially*) You'd had a drop in, hadn't you?

HIGGINS (*Peremptorily*) Sit down.

ELIZA Oh, if you're going to make a compliment of it—

HIGGINS (*Thundering at her*) Sit down.

MRS PEARCE (*Severely*) Sit down, girl. Do as you're told.

PICKERING (*Gently*) What is your name?

ELIZA Eliza Doolittle.

PICKERING Won't you sit down, Miss Doolittle?

ELIZA (*Coyly*) Oh, I don't mind if I do. (*She sits down on sofa*)

HIGGINS How much do you propose to pay me for the lessons?

ELIZA Oh, I know what's right. A lady friend of mine gets French lessons for heighteen pence an hour from a real French gentleman. Well, you wouldn't have the face to ask me the same for teaching me my own language as you would for French; so I won't give more than a shilling. Take it or leave it.

HIGGINS You know, Pickering, if you consider a shilling, not as a simple shilling, but as a percentage of this girl's income, it works out as fully equivalent to sixty or seventy pounds from a millionaire. By George, it's the biggest offer I ever had.

ELIZA (*Rising, terrified*) Sixty pounds! What are you talkin' about? I never offered you sixty pounds! Where would I get ...

HIGGINS Oh, hold your tongue.

ELIZA (*Weeping*) But I ain't got sixty pounds. Oh ...

MRS PEARCE Don't cry, you silly girl. Sit down. Nobody is going to touch your money.

HIGGINS Somebody is going to touch you with a broomstick, if you don't stop snivelling. Now, sit down.

ELIZA Aoooow! One would think you was my father!

HIGGINS If I decide to teach you, I'll be worse than two fathers to you. Here – (*He offers her his silk handkerchief*)

ELIZA What's this for?

HIGGINS To wipe your eyes. To wipe any part of your face that feels moist. Remember, that's your handkerchief; and that's your sleeve. Don't mistake the one for the other if you wish to become a lady in a shop.

PICKERING Higgins, I'm interested. What about your boast that you could pass her off as a duchess at the Embassy Ball? I'll say you're the greatest teacher alive if you can make that good. I'll bet you all the expenses of the experiment you can't do it. And I'll even pay for the lessons.

ELIZA Oh, you're real good. Thank you, Captain.

HIGGINS (*Tempted, looking at her*) It's almost irresistible. She's so deliciously low – so horribly dirty!

ELIZA Aoooow! I ain't dirty: I washed my face and hands afore I come, I did.

HIGGINS I'll take it! I'll make a duchess of this draggle-tailed guttersnipe!

ELIZA Aooooooow!

HIGGINS (*Carried away*) I'll start today! Now! This moment! Take her away and clean her, Mrs Pearce. Sandpaper if it won't come off any other way. Is there a good fire in the kitchen?

MRS PEARCE Yes, but—

HIGGINS (*Storming on*) Take all her clothes off and burn them.

Ring up and order some new ones. Wrap her up in brown paper till they come.

ELIZA You're no gentleman, you're not, to talk of such things. I'm a good girl, I am; and I know what the likes of you are, I do.

HIGGINS We want none of your slum prudery here, young woman. You've got to learn to behave like a duchess. Take her away, Mrs Pearce. If she gives you any trouble, wallop her.

ELIZA I'll call the police, I will!

MRS PEARCE But I've got no place to put her.

HIGGINS Put her in the dustbin.

ELIZA Aooooow!

PICKERING Oh come, Higgins! Be reasonable.

MRS PEARCE You must be reasonable, Mr Higgins, really you must. You can't walk over everybody like this.

HIGGINS *thus scolded subsides. The hurricane is succeeded by a zephyr of amiable surprise.*

HIGGINS (*With professional exquisiteness of modulation*) I walk over everybody? My dear Mrs Pearce, my dear Pickering. I never had the slightest intention of walking over anybody. All I propose is that we should be kind to this poor girl. If I did not express myself clearly it was because I did not wish to hurt her delicacy, or yours.

MRS PEARCE But, sir, you can't take a girl up like that as if you were picking up a pebble on the beach.

HIGGINS Why not?

MRS PEARCE Why not? But you don't know anything about her! What about her parents? She may be married.

ELIZA Garn!

HIGGINS There! As the girl very properly says: Garn!

ELIZA Who'd marry me?

HIGGINS (*Suddenly resorting to the most thrillingly beautiful low*

ELIZA   *tones in his best elocutionary style*) By George, Eliza, the streets will be strewn with the bodies of men shooting themselves for your sake before I've done with you.

ELIZA   Here! I'm goin' away! He's off his chump, he is. I don't want no balmies teachin' me.

HIGGINS   (*Wounded in his tenderest point by her insensibility to his elocution*) Oh, indeed! I'm mad, am I? Very well, Mrs Pearce, you needn't order the new clothes for her. Throw her out! (*He deftly retrieves his handkerchief*)

MRS PEARCE   Stop, Mr Higgins! I won't allow it. Go home to your parents, girl.

ELIZA   I ain't got no parents.

HIGGINS   There you are. 'She ain't got no parents.' What's all the fuss about? The girl doesn't belong to anybody, and she's no use to anybody but me. Take her upstairs and—

MRS PEARCE   But what's to become of her? Is she to be paid anything? Oh, do be sensible, sir.

HIGGINS   (*Impatiently*) What on earth will she want with money? She'll have her food and her clothes. She'll only drink if you give her money.

ELIZA   (*Turning on him*) Oh, you are a brute. It's a lie; nobody ever saw the sign of liquor on me. (*To* PICKERING) Oh, sir, you're a gentleman; don't let him speak to me like that!

PICKERING   (*In good-humoured remonstrance*) Does it occur to you, Higgins, that the girl has some feelings?

HIGGINS   (*Looking critically at her*) Oh, no, I don't think so. Not any feelings that we need bother about. (*Cheerily*) Have you, Eliza?

MRS PEARCE   Mr Higgins. I must know on what terms the girl is to be here. What is to become of her when you've finished your teaching? You must look ahead a little, sir.

HIGGINS   What's to become of her if I leave her in the gutter? Answer me that, Mrs Pearce.

MRS PEARCE That's her own business, not yours, Mr Higgins.
HIGGINS Well, when I've done with her, we can throw her back into the gutter, and then it will be her own business again: so that's all right. (*He is moved to a chuckle by his own little pleasantry*)
ELIZA Oh, you've no feelin' heart in you: you don't care for nothing but yourself. Here! I've had enough of this. I'm going. (*She makes for the door*)
HIGGINS (*Taking her by the arm*) Eliza! (*Snatching a chocolate cream from the table, his eyes suddenly twinkling with mischief*) Have some chocolates.
ELIZA (*Halting, tempted*) How do I know what might be in them? I've heard of girls being drugged by the like of you.

HIGGINS *breaks the chocolate in two, puts one half into his mouth and bolts it.*

HIGGINS Pledge of good faith, Eliza. I eat one half and you eat the other. (ELIZA *opens her mouth to retort.* HIGGINS *pops the chocolate into it*) You shall have boxes of them, barrels of them, every day. You shall live on them, eh?
ELIZA (*Her mouth full*) I wouldn't have ate it, only I'm too ladylike to take it out of me mouth.
HIGGINS (*Taking her by the hand and leading her up the stairs*) Think of it, Eliza. Think of chocolates, and taxis, and gold, and diamonds. (*They reach the balcony*)
ELIZA No! I don't want no gold and no diamonds. I'm a good girl, I am.
PICKERING Excuse me, Higgins, but I really must interfere! Mrs Pearce is quite right. If this girl is to put herself in your hands for six months for an experiment in teaching, she must understand thoroughly what she's doing!
HIGGINS (*Impressed with* PICKERING'*s logic, considers for a moment*) Eliza, you are to stay here for the next six months

learning how to speak beautifully, like a lady in a florist's shop. If you're good and do whatever you're told, you shall sleep in a proper bedroom and have lots to eat, and money to buy chocolates and take rides in taxis. If you're naughty and idle you will sleep in the back kitchen among the black beetles, and be walloped by Mrs Pearce with a broomstick. At the end of six months you shall go to Buckingham Palace in a carriage, beautifully dressed. If the King finds out you're not a lady, you will be taken by the police to the Tower of London where your head will be cut off as a warning to other presumptuous flower girls. If you are not found out, you shall have a present of seven-and-six to start life with as a lady in a shop. If you refuse this offer you will be the most ungrateful, wicked girl; and the angels will weep for you. (*To* PICKERING) Now are you satisfied, Pickering? (*To* MRS PEARCE) Could I put it more plainly or fairly, Mrs Pearce?

MRS PEARCE (*Resigned, starts up the stairs*) Come with me, Eliza.

HIGGINS That's right, Mrs Pearce. Bundle her off to the bathroom.

ELIZA (*Reluctantly and suspiciously*) You're a great bully, you are. I won't stay here if I don't like. And I won't let nobody wallop me.

MRS PEARCE Don't answer back, girl. (*She leads* ELIZA *through the door*)

ELIZA (*As she goes*) If I'd known what I was lettin' myself in for, I wouldn't have come up here. I've always been a good girl and I won't be put upon ... (*She follows* MRS PEARCE *out of the door*)

HIGGINS (*Coming down the stairs*) In six months – in three if she has a good ear and a quick tongue – I'll take her anywhere and pass her off as anything. I'll make a queen of that barbarous wretch.

Study activities

The Ants

1. To what extent does Tim know about his parents' separation? How does he feel about it?

2. All the speeches are very close to real life. Which ones particularly reveal how the characters are feeling?

3. Why do you think the author, Caryl Churchill, included Tim's fascination with ants and called the play *The Ants*?

4. In what ways does this play for radio differ from a stage play? Are there any moments that would work particularly well on the radio which would not be so effective on stage?

Separated Twins

1. Eddie and Mickey become friends very quickly when they first meet. Do you think the fact that they are actually twins somehow helped, or was it just chance?

2. What do you think the two women felt when Mrs Johnston handed over one of the babies to Mrs Lyons?

3. Write another short scene, imagining Mickey and his mother in their home the next day.

4. Many of the scenes are linked by a narrator, speaking in verse. The play starts with the narrator saying this:

STUDY ACTIVITIES

> So did you ever hear the tale of the Johnston twins,
> As like each other as two new pins;
> Of one womb born, on the self same day,
> How one was kept, one given away?
>
> Did you ever hear tell of that young mother
> Who stood and watched brother parted from brother;
> Who saw her children wrenched apart,
> That woman, with a stone in place of a heart?
>
> Then bring her on, come on let's see
> The author of such cruelty.
> And judge for ourselves this terrible sin.
> Bring on the mother, let the story begin.

Imagine the first meeting between the brothers is followed by a narrator speech, and write it in the same verse pattern.

5 The play was commissioned to be toured round schools and performed on the floor of a school hall. How would you arrange the staging of these scenes?

Who Is the True Mother?

1 After the first escape from the Ironshirts, Grusha says to the baby: 'I wouldn't be without you any more' (page 33), yet she had no intention of keeping the child originally. What has changed her attitude and made her so certain?

2 Do you have any sympathy for the governor's wife at any point in these scenes?

3 In the trial, the rogue judge, Azdak, makes many unconventional comments which are strange but have a

STUDY ACTIVITIES

ring of human truth to them. Quote some of these remarks and explain them and their place in the trial.

4 *The Caucasian Chalk Circle* has been one of the most internationally popular plays of the mid-twentieth century. Can you account, on the basis of these scenes, for why it has appealed to audiences in so many countries?

Death in the Barn

1 Tragedy comes from the way these children behave. What leads some young people, most often boys, to act in this kind of way?

2 Which of the boys would have been the most likely to have prevented the disaster? What are his characteristics?

3 This is a television play, as is the *Steptoe* episode that follows. Give examples of ways in which the form and writing of the play are affected by this.

4 If you were the director, where would you use close-ups, and what effect would you be aiming at?

Put the Old Man Away

1 What are Harold's motives for wanting to find an old people's home for his father? Is Harold being selfish or helpful?

2 This is from one episode in a television *series*, that has the same characters in a self-contained story each week. Pick out threads of this episode that could be brought back into later ones. Describe them. Choose one and write a scene about it for a later episode.

3 How well do you think the Matron managed the reception of Albert? Rewrite the last moments from when she comes in (page 72) with a different kind of person as Matron.

The Hundred Nights

1 Komachi is wretched. How would the audience get their overall impression of her present condition?

2 Can you imagine serious regrets for past actions? Write a short play in this style for chorus and the regretful central character in which he or she explores the memories of a painful past.

3 Can you find any moment or point of style in any other scenes in this volume or in other twentieth-century plays in which techniques similar to those in this play are to be found? Describe them.

Farewell to the Memories of Life

1 What is your impression of Johnson's life from these acted-out memories? What is it about the meetings that is satisfying to Johnson?

2 Invent one more memory for Johnson that he might well have had. Write another short memory scene that brings a key person from his past into this inn for him to meet.

STUDY ACTIVITIES

3 The author, J. B. Priestley, wrote of this play that he wanted to 'break away from the flavourless patter of modern realistic dialogue'. Select some examples of the dialogue that are clearly not 'realistic' and describe in what ways they are different and what effect they would have on an audience.

4 Imagine this play being staged: to what extent would you want to have realistic details and to what extent make the characters and the setting a fantasy? Give some examples of costumes, acting, the scenery and the styles that you would use.

Fighting Filth and Disease

1 Where do you stand in judging Dr Stockmann and the Mayor? Which would you support?

2 What kinds of things nowadays do some people think should be kept secret and why? How would you argue for or against such secrecy?

3 Dr Stockmann and the Mayor talk together for five pages before Petra breaks in. If you were directing this scene, what would you make the two actors do? When should they sit, when stand and when move?

4 Write a scene in which Petra and her mother discuss what they have heard between Dr Stockmann and his brother the Mayor.

STUDY ACTIVITIES

The Mystery of Goodness

1. How can you tell that Captain Vere admires Billy and distrusts the Master-at-Arms, John Claggart?

2. Was the trial fair? Could they have let Billy off?

3. This is a libretto, written to be sung. Choose some phrases that you consider would be especially effective sung. What is it about the wording that makes you think this?

4. The opera does not have the scene in which Vere tells Billy of the verdict: it cuts from Vere's solo to Billy's solo the next morning. Write a short scene that could go in between.

5. Listen to these scenes in a recording of the opera. Describe places in which the orchestra and singing make the effect stronger and any in which they make it less clear. (Recommended recording, conducted by Benjamin Britten, published on CD in 1989: 417 428 2 LH3.)

6. Scene 4, the last full scene in the opera, has all the crew singing on deck. How could you stage this in an opera house?

Death of a Martyr

1. Describe one or more twentieth-century situations in which people holding a religious faith find themselves as Thomas did, torn between the demands of those who rule the country and the demands of their religious beliefs.

2. Which speeches are in rhyming verse? What effect does this have?

STUDY ACTIVITIES

3 In the argument between the knights and Thomas how realistic do you consider the dialogue to be and in what ways is it not realistic?

4 On the evidence of this scene do you think Thomas wanted to be a martyr?

5 What kind of scenery would you use if you were producing this play in a theatre not a cathedral?

Talk More Genteel

1 Is Higgins being reasonable or inhuman?

2 How can the audience tell that Eliza has drive and determination?

3 To what extent does the way people speak affect how they are treated these days?

4 Below are the lyrics of a song that comes before this scene. Imagine a song that could be sung after this scene. Write the lyrics.

ELIZA   Garn!

HIGGINS   *Garn! I ask you, sir, what sort of word is that?*
It's 'Aooow' and 'Garn' that keep her in her place.
Not her wretched clothes and dirty face.

Why can't the English teach their children how to speak?
This verbal class distinction by now should be antique.
If you spoke as she does, sir,
Instead of the way you do,
Why, you might be selling flowers, too.

PICKERING   I beg your pardon!

HIGGINS   *An Englishman's way of speaking absolutely classifies him.*
The moment he talks he makes some other Englishman despise him.

One common language I'm afraid we'll never get.
Oh, why can't the English learn to set
A good example to people whose English is painful to your ears?
The Scotch and the Irish leave you close to tears.

There even are places where English completely disappears.
In America, they haven't used it for years!
Why can't the English teach their children how to speak?
Norwegians learn Norwegian; the Greeks are taught their Greek.
In France every Frenchman knows his language from 'A' to 'Zed'.
The French never care what they do, actually, as long as they pronounce it properly.

Arabians learn Arabian with the speed of summer lightning.
The Hebrews learn it backwards, which is absolutely frightening.
But use proper English, you're regarded as a freak.
Oh, why can't the English,
Why can't the English learn to speak?

Overview

1 All the scenes have key characters. Compare the key characters in three or four different plays. How has the writer chosen to show the important aspects of those characters? How would actors and directors make sure the audience interpreted the characters with full understanding?

STUDY ACTIVITIES

2 Contrast a play that uses only naturalistic dialogue with one that mostly uses heightened speech and verse. What are the advantages and disadvantages for each? How does the choice of styles of dialogue affect the way the scenes work?

3 Which plays have used different forms of commentators: 'narrator', 'voice', 'chorus'? How has this affected the telling of the story and the impact on the audience?

4 Consider the settings of the plays. Choose a few and describe what are the most important aspects of the setting for those scenes, and how they could be managed on a stage.

5 If you were to choose one of these for performance in your school, which would you choose? Why? How would you stage it?

The authors

Bertolt Brecht (1898–1956). Perhaps Germany's greatest dramatist, Brecht was born in Augsburg. When he was nineteen, in the last year of the First World War, Brecht began to study medicine at Munich University. Soon he was called up and served as a medical orderly in the army. That was a horrifying experience for him. His revulsion from fighting can be felt through all of his writings. A further result of this experience was that he was attracted to the views of the Communist party. His first important job was as drama critic for a newspaper, but soon after he joined a theatre in Munich as one of the advisers on the choice of plays. Over the next few years he wrote a number of plays himself, and published many of his poems. He moved to California in 1940. As an exile in America, he wrote his greatest plays: *Mother Courage, The Life of Galileo, The Good Woman of Setzuan, Herr Puntila and His Man Matti* and, in 1941–4, *The Caucasian Chalk Circle*. Brecht returned to Europe in 1947, and died in Berlin in the year that his company first appeared in London, when at last his influence began to be felt in the British theatre.

Caryl Churchill (1938–). Born in London, the only child of a cartoonist and a fashion model, Caryl Churchill moved to Canada with her parents when she was ten, where she started making up plays and writing stories: she remembers producing 'living-room pantomimes'. By fourteen she had written a full-length story, then she returned to England to go to Oxford University. She wrote a radio play and two stage plays that were produced by students, one of which was in verse, while the other included songs. All three plays also tried out the use of a narrator and unusual ways of presenting the action through stylised rather than naturalistic acting. Her greatest commercial success has been *Serious Money*, a 1987 satire on the world of get-rich-quick financiers.

T. S. Eliot (1888–1965) is best known as one of the twentieth century's greatest poets. Born in Missouri, in the United States, he studied at Harvard University and then Paris. A travelling scholarship brought him to Oxford, and the American poet Ezra Pound persuaded him to stay in England. He became a British citizen in 1927. He taught in two schools for a short while, and then worked for eight years in Lloyds Bank, before becoming a director of the literature publishing firm of Faber and Faber. His first publication of poetry was *Prufrock and Other Observations* in 1917. Five years later *The Waste Land* was published, and in 1944 *The Four Quartets*, both twentieth-century classics. He became a member of the Church of England, and his *Murder in the Cathedral* was commissioned for the annual Canterbury Cathedral Festival of 1935. Later Eliot wrote other verse plays, using ancient Greek plays as his basis, giving them modern naturalistic settings and styles: *The Family Reunion* (1939), *The Cocktail Party* (1949), *The Elder Statesman* (1958).

E. M. Forster (1879–1970) and Eric Crozier (1914–94). E. M. Forster was one of England's greatest twentieth-century novelists and critics. *Billy Budd* is his only dramatic work, written after persuasion by his friend, the composer Benjamin Britten. *The Longest Journey* (1907), *Where Angels Fear to Tread* (1905), *A Room with A View* (1908) and *A Passage to India* (1924) are his best-known novels. Eric Crozier directed plays in the pioneering early days of television from 1936 to 1939. He then directed operas, including Benjamin Britten's *Peter Grimes* for the reopening of Sadlers Wells and the post-war launch of British opera in

1945, a new dawn of a period in which English opera would flourish in its own right. Later he wrote the libretto for Britten's *Albert Herring* (1947) and *The Little Sweep* (1949). He also played an important part in the direction and organisation of the Aldeburgh Festival of Music and the Arts.

Ray Galton (1930–) and Alan Simpson (1929–). Both comedy writers in their own right, Galton and Simpson are best known for their forty or so 'Steptoe and Son' television scripts, about which they have written:

> Steptoe & Son were born in March 1962. They started life as one playlet in a series called *Comedy Playhouse* that we were writing at the time. Subsequently they were the subjects of five further series of programmes, until at the time of writing, thirty-four separate episodes concerning their adventures have been seen. We had no preconceived ideas of how the series would develop. Having first decided on their occupation, we then considered their relationship. Were they to be unrelated partners, two brothers, friends of the same age? We finally decided on father and son, which is just as well, otherwise we would have had to think up a new title. The next question was how old would they be? We decided to make the son in his late thirties as this would heighten the tragic element in the situation of a son still tied to a dependent parent. If the son had been a young man one would have the feeling that his life was still in front of him, that there was hope that he would eventually get away and create a new life for himself. Furthermore this happened to be our own age as well, and a writer is always at his best writing about things and people he is familiar with.

Henrik Ibsen (1828–1906). Ibsen's plays powerfully changed the style of European theatre. The son of a wealthy merchant who went bankrupt, he started work as a chemist's assistant, intending to study medicine. He wrote his first play then, which was rejected. He worked next as a journalist, and then in a theatre as stage director and resident playwright. When he moved to Oslo in 1862 he started writing on the life of the time, and *Love's Comedy* was a success. He visited Italy and Germany and then settled in Rome where he wrote his great poetic drama *Brand* (1865), followed by the famous verse play *Peer Gynt* (1867). The four plays that followed are the core of the development of his realistic work. Major themes of truth and deceit were set out in portrayals of the small-mindedness of town life: *Pillars of Society* (1877), a study of public life based on a lie; *A Doll's House* (1879), showing the destruction of domestic life by another lie; *Ghosts* (1881), the lingering poison of a lie in a marriage; and *An Enemy of the People* (1882), in which a man of truth is in conflict with the lies of society. Throughout Europe and America his plays, with realistic acting and stage management, had a major impact on the dominant naturalism of later play, film and television.

Alan Jay Lerner (1918–86) was born in the United States of America and graduated from Harvard University in 1940. He wrote two shows and hoped to work for Broadway theatres. He started by writing radio scripts. Then, in collaboration with the musician Frederick Loewe, he wrote in one week a musical, *What's Up* (1943). In 1945 he wrote *The Day Before Spring*, and in 1947 the successful *Brigadoon*. He then collaborated with the jazz composer who had worked with Brecht, Kurt Weill, on *Love Life*, and wrote the screenplay for the film *An American in Paris*. In 1951 he and Loewe had another success with *Paint Your Wagon*. The stage version of *My Fair Lady* was first presented in England at the Theatre Royal, Drury Lane, in April 1958. The world-famous film followed soon after.

THE AUTHORS

Dennis Potter (1935–94). Although he wrote successful stage plays, Dennis Potter is primarily thought of as one of the western world's leading television dramatists, with about thirty scripts to his credit. After a working-class upbringing and Oxford University, he tried journalism and politics. He had a major success with *Vote, Vote, Vote for Nigel Barton* (1965) and his study of Christ as a man who had to struggle with his own doubts in *Son of Man* (1969). His subjects were often controversial and he was technically innovative: *Pennies from Heaven* (1978) required the actors to mime to popular songs of the 1920s and 1930s that intercut the action; *Blue Remembered Hills* (1979), a memory play, required the adult actors to impersonate children. He called his new approach to television drama 'non-naturalism': a deliberate turning away from the reality of chronological narrative to unfettered leaps of the imagination, and the uninhibited use of time. *The Singing Detective* in 1986 was a painful screen drama, in which Potter used his own battles against disease.

J. B. Priestley (1894–1984) was born in Bradford, the son of a schoolmaster. On leaving school he went to work in the local wool trade, and at the age of sixteen he was already writing pieces for Bradford newspapers. He served in the army throughout the war of 1914–18, and on demobilisation in 1919 he was awarded a government grant which enabled him to go to Cambridge University. He was a literary critic and essayist before he began to write novels, and in 1929 everybody was reading and praising *The Good Companions*, which made him famous all over the world. Over the next thirty years this was followed by a score of successful novels. When he was forty, he started writing for the stage. He wrote about his new direction:

> As a youth I was a passionate playgoer, and for a time was determined to go on the stage myself . . . After twenty years

or so I found myself thinking hard about the Theatre again; but this time, being a professional writer, as a dramatist . . . I came to see that the Theatre, though much of its appeal may be childish, is an institution that cannot be safely despised even by a philosopher. It is indeed one of the few common meeting places of the child and the wise adult. It is rich in symbols.

In many of his plays he wrote in a realistic and naturalistic style, but in others, such as *Johnson Over Jordan*, he used the artifice of the theatre to blend naturalism with fantasy.

Willy Russell (1947–). Of his early childhood just outside Liverpool, Willy Russell wrote: 'My dad worked in a factory (later, having come to hate factory life, he got out and bought a chip shop) and my mother worked in a warehouse.' His secondary school was in an area that frightened him, Huyton, of which he wrote: 'Playtime was nothing to do with play; it was about survival. Thugs roamed the concrete and casually destroyed anything that couldn't move fast enough.' After pretty well complete failure at the school subjects, his mother persuaded him to learn to be a hairdresser, a job he then had for six years. It was then that he discovered his love of writing: 'Eventually I even had my own small salon and it was there that on slack days I would retire to the back room and try to do the one and only thing I felt I understood, felt that I could do, write.' To find a way of writing he managed to pass two examinations at evening classes, and gained a place in a college. To pay for that he worked as a factory cleaner, working dangerously on the oily roof girders. In the early 1970s he started playwriting. Along with *Blood Brothers*, *Educating Rita* has been the most successful, voted 'best comedy of the year' when produced by the Royal Shakespeare Company.

● Further reading

These suggestions are of plays or play collections that relate to the scenes in this selection, especially emphasising drama in performance (setting, direction, acting and interpretation of character), variety of forms (television, stage musical, opera) and different uses of language.

At the Hawk's Well and other plays by W.B. Yeats (Macmillan)
Blood Brothers by Willy Russell
The 'Caine' Mutiny Court-Martial by Herman Wouk
The Caucasian Chalk Circle by Bertolt Brecht
Death of a Salesman by Arthur Miller
The Diary of Anne Frank by Frances Goodrich and Albert Hackett
Educating Rita by Willy Russell (Longman Literature)
A Kind of Loving by Stan Barstow and Alfred Bradley
The Life of Galileo by Bertolt Brecht
The Long and the Short and the Tall by Willis Hall
The Moon of the Caribbees and six other plays of the sea by Eugene O'Neill (Jonathan Cape)
Murder in the Cathedral by T.S. Eliot
Noah's Flood (extract from the medieval play) in *Landmarks* selected and edited by Linda Marsh (Longman Imprint Books)
Not Not Not Not Not Enough Oxygen and other plays by Caryl Churchill (Longman)
One Day, When I Was Lost by James Baldwin
Pygmalion by Bernard Shaw (Longman Literature)
Saint Joan by Bernard Shaw (Longman Literature)
A Sleep of Prisoners by Christopher Fry
Spring and Port Wine by Bill Naughton

Three Plays: A Doll's House, Ghosts, The Wild Duck by Henrik Ibsen (Longman Literature)
The Winslow Boy by Terence Rattigan (Longman Literature)

Operas and musicals

My Fair Lady by Alan Jay Lerner, music Frederick Loewe
Peter Grimes, libretto Montague Slater, music Benjamin Britten
The Prodigal Son, libretto William Plomer, music Benjamin Britten
West Side Story, book Arthur Laurents, lyrics Stephen Sondheim, music Leonard Bernstein

Television

P'Tang, Yang, Kipperbang and other TV plays by Jack Rosenthal (Longman Imprint Books)
The TV Script of Buddy by Nigel Hinton (Heinemann)

Collections

Cross Winds, an anthology of black dramatists in the diaspora edited by William Branch (Indiana University Press)
Plays for Today (Longman Caribbean Writers)
Ten Short Plays selected and edited by Geoff Barton (Longman Imprint Books)
Theatre Choice compiled by Michael Marland (Student Drama, Nelson)

Addison Wesley Longman Limited
Edinburgh Gate, Harlow,
Essex CM20 2JE, England.
and Associated Companies throughout the world.

© Addison Wesley Longman Limited 1996
All rights reserved; no part of this publication
may be reproduced, stored in a retrieval system,
or transmitted in any form or by any means, electronic,
mechanical, photocopying, recording, or otherwise,
without either the prior written permission of the
Publishers or a licence permitting restricted copying
issued by the Copyright Licensing Agency Ltd,
90 Tottenham Court Road, London W1P 9HE.

This educational edition first published 1996

Editorial material set in 10/12.5 pt Stone Sans
Produced by Longman Singapore Publishers (Pte) Ltd
Printed in Singapore

ISBN 0 582 25394 2

Cover illustration by John Clenentson

The publisher's policy is to use paper manufactured from
sustainable forests

Acknowledgements

We are grateful to the following for permission to reproduce scenes from plays:

Boosey & Hawkes Music Publishers Ltd for an extract from *Billy Budd*, the libretto by E M Forster and Eric Crozier for the opera by Benjamin Britten (1951) © Copyright 1951 by Hawkes & Son (Ltd); Faber & Faber Ltd for an extract from *Murder in the Cathedral* by T S Eliot (1935); the authors' agent for an extract from 'Homes Fit for Heroes' in *Steptoe and Son* by Ray Galton and Alan Simpson; the author's agent for an extract from *An Enemy of the People* by Henrik Ibsen translated by Michael Meyer in *Ibsen Plays: Book Two*; International Music Publications Ltd and The Estate of Alan Jay Lerner for 'Talk More Genteel' (Lerner/Loewe) from the musical *My Fair Lady* © 1996 Chappell & Co Inc, USA, Warner/Chappell Music Ltd, London W1Y 3FA/Copyright 1956 by Alan Jay Lerner and Frederick Loewe, copyright renewed; Penguin Books Ltd for an extract from 'The Ants' by Caryl Churchill from *New English Dramatists 12: Radio Plays* (1968) copyright © Caryl Churchill, 1968; the author's agent on behalf of PFH (Overseas) Ltd for the extract 'Death in the Barn' from *The Blue Remembered Hills* by Dennis Potter © Dennis Potter, 1984, 1996; the author's agent for an extract from *Johnson Over Jordan* by J B Priestley (1939); Reed Consumer Books Ltd for extracts from *The Caucasian Chalk Circle* by Bertolt Brecht translated by James and Tanya Stern and W H Auden (Methuen) and *Blood Brothers* by Willy Russell (Methuen).